QUIET MOMENTS
WITH GOD

FOR MOTHERS

RACINE, WI

Quiet Moments with God for Mothers
ISBN: 979-8-88898-078-1 - *Paperback*
ISBN: 979-8-88898-079-8 - *Hardcover*
ISBN: 979-8-88898-080-4 - *Ebook*
Copyright © 2023 by Honor Books

Cover design by Faille Schmitz.

INTRODUCTION

Quiet moments—for personal meditation, for fellowship with God—we need both in order to live balanced lives while meeting the complex demands of motherhood.

In a world that is moving and swirling past us with great speed and intensity, it's tempting to put those quiet times aside and regard them as luxuries rather than necessities. But the truth is—moments of quiet tranquility are critical. They help us define our relationships, our roles, our priorities, and ourselves. Without them, we become slaves to our lifestyles rather than the masters of them.

We hope you will find that the devotionals in this book help you make your quiet moments productive and inspiring. We have selected those that relate specifically to the issues mothers face. And we have made them short enough to fit easily into your special time apart yet long enough to provide a solid kick-off for your day. As you read, we hope that they will draw you closer to God.

FIRST CUP

Many people wouldn't dream of starting their day without a cup of coffee. They count on that "first cup of the day" to wake them up and get them going.

There are others who have discovered an even more potent day-starter: first-thing-in-the-morning prayer.

For some, this is a prayer voiced to God before getting out of bed. For others, it is a planned time of prayer between getting dressed and leaving for work. For still others, it is a commitment to get to work half an hour early to spend quiet, focused time in prayer before the workday begins.

Henry Ward Beecher, one of the most notable preachers of the last century, had this to say about starting the day with prayer:

In the morning, prayer is the key that opens to us the treasure of God's mercies and blessings. The first act of the soul in early morning should be a draught at the heavenly fountain. It will sweeten the taste for the day.

. . . And if you tarry long so sweetly at the throne, you will come out of the closet as the high priest of Israel came from the awful ministry at the altar of incense, suffused all over with the heavenly fragrance of that

6

communion.[1]

A popular song in Christian groups several years ago read, "Fill my cup, Lord; I lift it up, Lord. Come and quench this thirsting of my soul. Bread of heaven, feed me till I want no more; Fill my cup, fill it up and make me whole."[2]

Morning prayer is a time to have your cup filled to overflowing with peace. Then, as you have contact with other people at home and at work, you can pour that same peace into them. And the good news is — unlimited free refills are readily available any time your cup becomes empty throughout the day!

Without prayer, no work is well begun.

BOOK OF WISDOM

TODAY'S SURE THING

In his book for children, *The Chance World*, Henry Drummond describes a place in which nothing is predictable. The sun may rise, or it may not. The sun might suddenly appear at any hour, or the moon might rise instead of the sun. When children are born in Drummond's fantasy world, they might have one head or a dozen heads, and their head or heads may not be positioned between their shoulders.

> The steps of a good man are ordered by the Lord.
>
> PSALM 37:23
> NKJV

If one jumps into the air in the "chance world," it is impossible to predict whether the person will come down again. That the person came down yesterday is no guarantee he or she will come down the next time. All the natural laws change from hour to hour.

Today, a child's body might be so light it is impossible for him or her to descend from a chair to the floor. Tomorrow, the same child might descend with great force, landing near the center of the earth.

In the final analysis, *The Chance World* is a frightening world. While most people enjoy a certain amount of spontaneity in their lives, they enjoy life more when it is lived against a backdrop of predictability, surety, and trustworthiness.

The Scriptures promise us that the Lord changes not. He is the same yesterday, today, and forever. (See Hebrews 13:8.) Furthermore, His natural laws do not change unless He authorizes their change for the good of His people. His commandments do not change. His promises to us are sure promises. We can know with certainty, "The steps of a good man are ordered by the Lord" (Psalm 37:23 NKJV).

The Lord may have some surprises for you today. They are a part of His ongoing creation in your life. But His surprises are always custom-designed for you on the rock-solid foundation of His love. It is always His desire that you experience the highest and best in your life. You can count on Him!

All but God is changing day by day.

CHARLES KINGSLEY

SHARE THE SECRET

A woman named Frances once knew a young person at church named Debbie. Debbie always seemed effervescent and happy, although Frances knew she had faced struggles in her life. Her long-awaited marriage had quickly ended in divorce, and she had struggled to get a grip on her single life. She hadn't chosen it, but she decided she would live it with utmost enjoyment and satisfaction. Debbie was active in Sunday school, in the choir, and in the church renewal movement. She was also a leader of the junior high girls' group.

> I have learned the secret of being content.
>
> PHILIPPIANS 4:12

Frances enjoyed knowing Debbie because her whole face seemed to smile, and she always greeted Frances with a hug. One day she asked Debbie, "How is it that you are always so happy—you have so much energy, and you never seem to get down?"

With her eyes smiling, Debbie said, "I know the secret!"

"What secret is that? What are you talking about?" Frances asked.

Debbie replied, "I'll tell you all about it, but you have to promise to share the 'secret' with others."

Frances agreed, "Okay, now what is it?"

"The secret is this: I have learned there is little I can

do in my life that will make me truly happy. I must depend on God to make me happy and meet my needs. When a need arises in my life, I have to trust God to supply according to His riches. I have learned most of the time I don't need half of what I think I do. He has never let me down. Since I learned that secret—I have been happy."

Frances' first thought was, *That's too simple!* But upon reflecting over her own life, she recalled how she thought a bigger house would make her happy—but it didn't! She thought a better-paying job would make her happy—but it hadn't. She realized her greatest happiness was found sitting on the floor with her grandchildren, eating pizza and watching a movie—a simple gift from God.

Debbie knew the secret; Frances learned the secret; and now you know it too!

Teach us to put our trust in thee and to
await thy helping hand.

TRADITIONAL AMISH PRAYER

THE "TO-BE LIST"

Nearly all of us face our day with a "to-do list." The Scriptures compel us, however, to have a "to-be list."

While it may be important to accomplish certain tasks, engage in certain projects, or have certain encounters during a day, what is more important for *eternity* is the person we *are* throughout the day.

From a "to-do" perspective, we tend to come before the Lord and say, "This is my list, and this is my schedule. Please be with me, help me, and bless me."

From a "to-be" perspective, we might make these requests of the Lord:

- Help me to reflect Your love today.

- Help me to display Your joy.

- Help me to manifest Your peace.

- Help me to practice Your patience.

- Help me to express Your kindness.

- Help me to make known Your goodness.

When the holy spirit controls our lives he will produce this kind of fruit in us: love, joy, peace, patience, kindness, goodness, faithfulness, gentleness, and self-control.

GALATIANS 5:22-23 TLB

- Help me to reveal Your faithfulness.
- Help me to show Your gentleness.
- Help me to exhibit Your self-control.

Wishful thinking does not produce these traits, however. They come from a life lived in communication with the Lord. They are the distinguishing marks of His presence in our lives. Our "to-be" list, therefore, must always begin with an invitation to the Holy Spirit to inspire us and impel us toward good works.

In order to *express* the Lord's kindness, for example, we first must see ourselves as *receiving* the Lord's kindness. In receiving His kindness, we become much more attuned to opportunities in which we might show His kindness to others. "Being kind" becomes a part of everything we do. The way we do our chores, hold our meetings, run our errands, and engage in our projects display His kindness to those around us.

When we make our "to-be" list our top priority, the things we have "to do" become much more obvious—and far less burdensome!

He who labors as he prays lifts his heart
to God with his hands.

SAINT BERNARD

EVERYDAY BENEFITS

Blessings we take for granted are often forgotten. Yet every day God "loads us with benefits." This morning think of some common things you may have taken for granted—and thank God for them:

> Blessed be the Lord, who daily loads us with benefits.
>
> PSALM 68:19 NKJV

- Lungs that work well and steadily—ten to fifteen times each minute

- Bones that protect vital organs and the muscles that hold them in their place

- A healthy disease-fighting immune system

- An untiring heart that pumps nine pints of blood through a sixty-thousand-mile network of vessels

- A body temperature that remains constant

- Our five senses—eyes to see the dawn, ears to hear your loved one's voice, a nose to smell the freshness of the early dew, the sense of touch to enjoy a hug, and the sense of taste to savor breakfast

- Nerve cells that synapse and send messages to other parts of the body

- A digestive system that brings nourishment to all the cells of the body

- The ability—and desire—to get up and out of bed

in the morning

• A place to live and a place to work

• Loving and supportive family, friends, and colleagues and the opportunities to let them know you care about them

• An intimate relationship with God through Jesus Christ

• The changing seasons that remind us of the different times of our lives

• Each day's unique beauty — the angle of the sun, white clouds stretched out across the blue afternoon sky, the gold and pink sunset

• The rotation of the earth that gives us day and night

• Times for quiet reflection and grateful remembrances

• The gift of laughter — and the ability to laugh at our mistakes

Add your own blessings to this list, and keep it growing all day long![3]

Reflect upon your present blessings, of
which everyone has many.

CHARLES DICKENS

TRUE VALUE

"The last will be first, and the first will be last."

MATTHEW
20:16

In the J. M. Barrie play *The Admirable Crichton*, the Earl of Loam, his family, and several friends are shipwrecked on a desert island. These nobles were adept at chattering senselessly, playing bridge, and scorning poorer people. However, they could not build an outdoor fire, clean fish, or cook food—the very skills they needed to survive.

Stranded on a desert island, what the Earl's family and friends did know was entirely useless for their survival. Had it not been for their resourceful butler Crichton, they would have starved to death. He was Ae only one who possessed the basic skills to sustain life.

In a great turnabout, Crichton became the group's chief executive officer. He taught the Earl and his family and friends the skills they needed, and he organized their efforts to ensure their survival until their rescue.

It is always good to remind ourselves of our "relative" place in society. If we are on top, we need to remember we can soon be at the bottom. If we perceive ourselves as at the bottom, we need to know that in God's order we are among "the first."

In *The Finishing Touch*, Chuck Swindoll raises the issue of perceived significance by asking about the people behind these Christian greats:

• Who taught Martin Luther his theology and inspired his translation of the New Testament?

• Who visited with Dwight L. Moody at a shoe store and spoke to him about Christ?

• Who was the elderly woman who prayed faithfully for Billy Graham for over twenty years?

• Who found the Dead Sea Scrolls?

• Who discipled George Mueller and snatched him from a sinful lifestyle?[4]

We may not achieve the fame and recognition from people that we would like to have in this life, but God doesn't call us to be well known or admired. He calls us to be faithful to Him in whatever situation we find ourselves. When we are, we can see more clearly when He promotes us and gives us favor with others.

When men cease to be faithful to their
God, he who expects to find them so to
each others will be much disappointed.

GEORGE HORNE

RUN WITH PERSEVERANCE

There may be no better feeling in the world than the joy of winning a race you were never expected to win!

Just ask Jenny Spangler. She won the women's marathon at the United States Olympic Trials in February on 1996, earning the right to compete at the Summer Olympic Games in Atlanta, Georgia.

At the time of the trials, Spangler was qualifier number 61, which meant that sixty runners had entered the race with faster times than hers. No one had ever heard of her—and no one thought she could maintain a winning pace when she passed the leaders at the sixteen-mile mark.

Spangler had few successes to her credit. She had set an American junior record in the marathon during college, but then she left the sports scene after a stress fracture dashed her hopes in the Olympic Trials of 1984. Abandoning the sport after she ran poorly in 1988, she returned to school and earned a master's degree in business administration. She ran only two marathons be-

> Therefore, since we are surrounded by such a great cloud of witnesses, let us throw off everything that hinders and the sin that so easily entangles. And let us run with perseverance the race marked out for us . . .
>
> HEBREWS 12:1

tween 1988 and 1996.

At the marathon trials, she was such an unknown that the second and third-place finishers asked each other, "Who is she?" after she took the lead and held on to it.

The favorites in February's race expected Spangler to fade, but she never did. Somewhere inside herself, she found the courage and stamina to finish strong. Not only did she make the Olympic team, but she also took home first prize — forty-five thousand dollars.

Does the day ahead of you look as grueling as a marathon? Keep Jenny Spangler in mind as you jog through your various commitments and responsibilities. Believe you can get the job done. Run the race God has marked out before you. Keep moving! You can end each day with the satisfaction of knowing you are that much closer to the goal!

Today, whatever may annoy, the word for
me is joy, simple joy.

JOHN KENDRICKS BANGS

ON THE ROAD AGAIN

Getting yourself out of bed in the morning is one thing. Feeling prepared to face whatever comes your way that day is another. Where do you turn for a confidence-booster? Believe it or not, one of the best confidence-builders you can find may be inside those fuzzy slippers you like to wear: your own two feet.

> God did not give use a spirit of timidity, but a spirit of power, of love, and of self-discipline.
>
> 2 TIMOTHY 1:7

Researchers have discovered that regular exercise — thirty minutes, three or four times a week — boosts the confidence level of both men and women. This is due in part to the way exercise strengthens, tones, and improves the body's appearance. It also has to do with brain chemistry.

When a person exercises, changes take place inside the brain. Endorphins, released as one exercises, are proteins that work in the pleasure centers of the brain and make a person feel more exhilarated. When the heart rate increases during exercise, neurotrophins are also released, causing a person to feel more alert and focused.

Are you feeling anxious about your day? Take a walk, jog, cycle, or do some calisthenics first thing in the morning. See if you don't feel a little more on top of the world.

Those who exercise regularly also feel that if they can discipline themselves to exercise, they can discipline themselves to do just about anything!

The human body is one of the most awesome examples of God's creative power — an example we live with daily. He has created us not only to draw confidence from reading His Word and experiencing His presence through prayer, but also from the use of our body.

Put on those walking shoes and talk with God as you go! Not only will your body become more fit and your mind more alert, but the Holy Spirit will give you direction and peace about your day.

Walking and talking with God is great
soul exercise!

UNKNOWN

WHERE DOES THE TIME GO?

Most of us can look around and find reminders of good intentions. We readily see areas where we never followed through to reach a goal. The seldom-used exercise equipment needs dusting. A piano, intended to fulfill our dreams of happy family sing-a-longs, sits silent. The books piled on the nightstand remain to be read. And the laptop computer we intended to take on vacation to write a novel is still in its original packaging.

> While it is daytime, we must continue doing the work of the One who sent me. Night is coming, when no one can work.
>
> JOHN 9:4 NCV

More importantly, there are the children in our family who wait for our attention. Every child has gifts and abilities waiting to be developed—but that takes time. To tap into potential takes intentional, concerted effort. It doesn't just happen. Time for meaningful interaction and activity doesn't always "appear" to us as we juggle a full day of appointments and other commitments.

The time God gives to us is ours to spend—we determine how to use it. We can fill it with life-building activities, or we can let it sift through our fingers hour by hour, day by day, week by week, until before we know it, an entire year is gone and very little accomplished.

As long as you are alive, your time—24 hours, 1,440 minutes, 86,400 seconds a day—*will* be spent. It is up to you to decide *how* you are going to spend it. Accept the challenge to make every moment count! When you take your child to the dentist, make it an adventure, a time to listen, learn, and share God's wisdom. Is there a free hour when you can sit quietly and read a chapter or two in one of those books?

Look at what you have planned for today, and set your priorities according to the goals you have set for your life. Do the same thing tomorrow and the next day. It won't be long before your life will begin to be more productive and more fulfilling.

———

We always have time enough, if we use it.

JOHANN WOLFGANG VON GOETHE

SEE THE LIGHT

> Thou art my lamp, O Lord; and the Lord illumines my darkness.
>
> 2 SAMUEL 22:29
> NASB

Helen Keller may have lost her ability to see, hear, and speak at a very early age, but she did not lose her gift of inspiring others. In her many books and through a world tour designed to promote the education of others who shared her disabilities, Keller spoke eloquently on the subject of darkness—the kind that invades the hearts and minds of the sighted:

> Truly I have looked into the very heart of darkness, and refused to yield to its paralyzing influence, but in spirit I am one of those who walk the morning. What if all dark, discouraging moods of the human mind come across my way as thick as the dry leaves of autumn? Other feet have traveled that road before me, and I know the desert leads to God as surely as the green, refreshing fields and fruitful orchards.

> I, too, have been profoundly humiliated, and brought to realize my littleness amid the immensity of creation. The more I learn, the less I think I know, and the more I understand of my sense-experience, the more I perceive its shortcomings and its inadequacy as a basis of life. Sometimes the points of view of the optimist and the pessimist are placed before me so skillfully balanced that only by sheer force of spirit can I keep my hold upon a practical, livable philosophy of life. But I use my will, choose life and reject its opposite—nothingness.[5]

When the day ahead of you seems shadowed or darkness threatens to overcome you, choose life! Take Helen Keller's words to heart and reject "nothingness" by turning to the Lord. He will bring light into your soul and joy into your heart.

'Tisn't life that matters! 'Tis the courage
your bring to it!

HUGH WALPOLE

GRACE FOR TODAY

I n *The Grace of Giving*, Stephen Olford gives an account of Peter Miller, a Baptist pastor who lived during the American Revolution. He lived in Ephrata, Pennsylvania, and enjoyed the friendship of George Washington.

> . . . for all have sinned and fall short of the glory of God, and all are justified freely by his grace through the redemption that came by Christ Jesus.
>
> ROMANS 3:23-24

Michael Wittman also lived in Ephrata. He was an evil-minded man who did all he could to oppose and humiliate the pastor. One day Michael Wittman was arrested for treason and sentenced to die. Peter Miller traveled the seventy miles to Philadelphia on foot to plead for the life of the traitor.

"No, Peter," General Washington said, "I cannot grant you the life of your friend."

"My friend!" exclaimed the old preacher. "He's the bitterest enemy I have."

"What?" exclaimed Washington. "You've walked seventy miles to save the life of an enemy? That puts the matter in a different light. I'll grant your pardon."

Peter Miller took Michael Wittman back home to Ephrata—no longer an enemy, but a friend.

Miller's example of grace and forgiveness flowed from his knowledge of God's sacrifice for the human race. Because God forgave him and sacrificed His Son for him, he found the grace to sacrifice for his enemy. Although most of us know God's grace and love for us is great, sometimes we have to be reminded that His love never fails — even when we do!

At the Pan American Games, a United States diver was asked how he coped with the stress of an international diving competition. He replied that he climbed to the board, took a deep breath, and thought, "Even if I blow this dive, my mother will still love me." Then he would strive for excellence.

At the beginning of each day, take a deep breath and say, "Even if I blow it today, my God will still love me." Then, assured of His grace and quickness to forgive, go into the day seeking a perfect score!

A mother's love endures through all.

WASHINGTON IRVING

MAKING CONNECTIONS

I n *Silent Strength for My Life*, Lloyd John Ogilvie tells the story of a young boy he met while traveling. He noticed the boy waiting alone in the airport lounge for his flight to be called. Boarding began for the flight, and the young child was sent ahead of the adult passengers to find his seat. When Ogilvie got on the aircraft, he discovered the boy had been assigned the seat next to his.

The boy was polite when Ogilvie engaged him in conversation and then quietly spent time coloring in an airline coloring book. He showed neither anxiety nor worry about the flight as preparation was made for takeoff.

> My help comes from the Lord, who made heaven and earth.
>
> PSALM 121:2 NKJV

During the flight, the plane flew into a very bad storm, which caused the jetliner to bounce around like a "kite in the wind." The air turbulence and subsequent pitching and lurching of the aircraft frightened some of the passengers, but the young boy seemed to take it all in stride.

A female passenger seated across the aisle from the boy became alarmed by the wild rolling of the aircraft. She asked the boy, "Little boy, aren't you scared?"

"No, Ma'am," he replied, looking up just briefly from his coloring book. "My dad's the pilot."

There are times when events in our lives make us feel like we are in the middle of a turbulent storm. Try as we might, we cannot seem to land on solid ground or get a sure footing. We may have the sensation of being suspended in mid-air with nothing to hold on to, nothing to stand on, and no sure way to get to safety.

In the midst of the storm, however, we can remember that our Heavenly Father is our Pilot. Despite the circumstances, our lives are in the hands of the One who created Heaven and earth.

If uncontrollable fear begins to rise within you today, say to yourself, "My Dad's the Pilot!"[6]

The pilot knows the unknown seas, and
he will bring us through.

JOHN OXENHAM

ENJOYING THE SCENERY

Every day has moments worth savoring and enjoying to the fullest. It may take some effort to search out those moments, but the reward is a sense of enriched meaning in life, which is, in turn, motivating and satisfying.

> The earth is full of the goodness of the Lord.
>
> PSALM 33:5
> NKJV

Watch your children scamper for the school bus. Play freely in a warm spring rain shower. Enjoy observing the movement of a caterpillar on a leaf. Take your brown-bag lunch to the park and watch the geese circle on the pond or the elderly men bowl on the green. Gaze out a window and watch the birds making their nest on a ledge or the careful balancing act of window washers at work on the building across the boulevard. Enjoy a steaming cup of cappuccino in a garden- room cafe while a string ensemble plays in the background. Watch puppies tumble about in their play or kittens toying with a ball of yarn. Linger at a balcony rail with a glass of tangy lemonade and watch the sun set in golden glory.

Harold V. Melchert once said:

> Live your life each day as you would climb a mountain. An occasional glance toward the summit keeps the goal in mind, but many beautiful scenes are to be observed from each new vantage point. Climb slowly, steadily, enjoying each passing moment; and the view

from the summit will serve as a fitting climax for the journey.

God's creation is all around us—not only in the form of foliage, animals, and birds, but also in people. Take time today to enjoy what God has done and is doing! You'll enjoy what you are doing more.

The kiss of the sun for pardon, the song of the birds for mirth, one is nearer God's heart in a garden then anywhere else on earth.

UNKNOWN

TAKING A STAND

Nine-year-old Kevin was upset at learning one of his favorite Popsicle flavors was being discontinued. But what's a kid going to do? Fighting City Hall when you're under voting age can seem like a fruitless endeavor.

"But you're a consumer," the boy's mother reminded him. "Yes, you can make a difference. You can start a protest. You can stand up and be counted." So Kevin took his mother's advice.

With the help of his cousins, he launched a petition drive, eventually gathering 130 signatures. The children also constructed picket signs with catchy sayings. Finally, on a rainy January day, Kevin and nearly a dozen family members marched at the Popsicle's headquarters.

The company's CEO saw the marchers from the window of his office and invited them inside. He listened to the children's pleas and then explained the company's position. Extensive marketing research had been done, and thousands of dollars had already been spent to present a new flavor. In the end, however, Kevin and his group won the day. The CEO decided to forget the new

Be strong and of a good courage, fear not, nor be afraid of them: for the Lord thy God, he it is that doth go with thee; he will not fail thee, nor forsake thee.

DEUTERONOMY 31:6

flavor and grant the petitioners' plea to return the old flavor to the marketplace.

Never give in to the notion that you are too insignificant to lead the move toward a positive change in your world. As a band leader once pointed out in an inspirational speech to a group of students: the smallest person in the band, the head twirler, is the one who is leading us down the street!

The Lord expects each of us to be bold enough to speak His truth whenever the opportunity arises. Sometimes truth is best expressed in conversations, letters, or face-to-face encounters. Sometimes truth may need to be expressed with placards and petitions. In either case, one person begins the process by deciding to take a stand. You can be that person today.

Obstacles will look large or small to you according to whether you are large or small.

ORISON SWETT MARDEN

SHAKE IT UP

Sometimes your daily routine can seem more like a never-ending rut. The activities and responsibilities that were once fresh and new gradually become stale and old. What can you do to shake things up a bit?

> Gird your minds for action.
>
> 1 PETER 1:13 NASB

A woman asked herself that question one morning as she arose at her usual time. She had done all she needed to do to get her children off to school and her husband to work. Now she was home alone, looking for the motivation to face her day.

She said to herself, *I know what I'll do. I'll turn things upside-down. Instead of sticking to my usual schedule, I'll reverse the order.*

That meant her first item of business was preparing dinner. She thought she might feel strange preparing meat and vegetables at 9 AM, but she was surprised to find she felt a sense of relief at having this "chore" done early. Somehow, it made the rest of the housework and errands less stressful.

She found a little extra time to write a letter and catch up on some reading, and by the time her children came tromping in from school, she felt happier than she had in weeks. She was already thinking of other ways to add variety to her daily routine. Who says you have to do the same things in the same way at the same time every day?

The Bible clearly tells us that our God is a God of

infinite variety! While His commandments are not negotiable, His methods often change. That's part of His nature as our Creator. The Lord is continually creating new methods to reach us with His love and to show us His care.

Break out of your rut today! Ask the Lord to give you insight into how you might participate more fully in His creative process by doing things differently

---

Variety's the very spice of life, that gives
it all it's flavour.

WILLIAM COWPER

AS TO THE LORD

When we think of the most noble professions, we nearly always think of those that offer a service, such as doctors, lawyers, or teachers. Perhaps at the pinnacle of the service professions are those who are involved in full-time ministry — the helping of others in their spiritual lives in the name of the Lord. We tend to revere most highly those who make a commitment to serving God and others: pastors, priests, monks, missionaries, evangelists, and Bible teachers.

> With good will render service, as to the Lord, and not to men.
>
> EPHESIANS 6:7 NASB

Ministry, however, is not limited to those who earn their living by it. Ministry is the call and challenge of God to all Christians. Ministry is giving to others and living our lives *as unto the Lord.*

Ministry happens in the home, in the school, on the street, at the grocery store, in the boardroom, at the committee meeting, and in the gym. It happens wherever and whenever a person, motivated by the love of Jesus Christ, performs an act of loving service for another person.

Gandhi once wrote:

> *If when we plunge our hand into a bowl of water,*
> *Or stir up the fire with the bellows*

Or tabulate interminable columns of figures on our bookkeeping table,

Or, burnt by the sun, we are plunged in the mud of the rice field,

Or standing by the smelter's furnace

We do not fulfill the same religious life as if in prayer in a monastery, the world will never be saved.[7]

There is no ignoble work except that which is void of ministry! There is no lack of meaning in any job performed with God's love and "as unto the Lord."

Whatever the tasks you face today, perform them as if you were performing them for Jesus himself, because ultimately you are!

Be satisfied with nothing but your best.

EDWARD ROWLAND SILL

LEADER OF THE PACK

B eing the owner of a small business is not easy. Just when you start to build a clientele, along comes a crafty competitor who copies your style or improves on your methods. Next thing you know, revenues are falling, and you find yourself looking over your shoulder, trying to avoid being hit by another wave of wanna-be's.

> See, the former things have taken place, and new things I declare; before they spring into being I announce them to you.
>
> ISAIAH 42:9

A man on the West Coast found himself in this situation. His first venture was commercial fishing. When larger companies took over the water, he began renting out small sailboats and kayaks to people who wanted to explore the bay. Soon others with stronger financial backing moved in on that business.

Once again, he needed a new idea. How about submarine tours? After doing some research, the entrepreneur realized the cost of buying and maintaining a sub was beyond his reach. But a semi-submersible underwater viewing boat was not! The boat looks like a sub, but it doesn't dive. Passengers can go below deck and view the fascinating world under the sea.8

When your income seems to be going out with the tide, you may need to be a little creative. Talk with other people, do some research, consider even the "crazy" ideas, and glean what you can from them. You never know which wave might be the one that carries you safely and profitably to the shore.

God's creative work didn't end with His creation of the world. He continues His work today by giving each of us a dose of creativity. He invites us to be part of His plan and purpose for the earth by using this creative energy. Your ideas are God's gift to you for your provision, prosperity, and the fulfillment of your purpose in life.

Ask the Lord to inspire you anew today. Ask Him to give you His next idea for your life!

Small opportunities are often the beginning of great enterprises.

DEMOSTHENES

BEARING FRUIT

Two brothers were out walking on their father's vast acreage when they came upon a peach tree, its branches heavy with fruit. Each brother ate several juicy, tree-ripened peaches. When they started toward the house, one brother gathered enough peaches for a delicious peach cobbler and several jars of jam. But the second brother cut a limb from the tree to start a new peach tree. When he got home, he carefully tended the tree-cutting until he could plant it outdoors. The branch took root and eventually produced healthy crops of peaches for him to enjoy year after year.

> Meditate upon these things; give thyself wholly to them; that thy profiting may appear to all.
>
> 1 TIMOTHY 4:15 KJV

The Bible is like the fruit-bearing tree. Hearing the Word of God is like the first brother. He gathered fruit from hearing the Word and had enough to take home with him to eat later. But that doesn't compare with having your own peach tree in the backyard. Memorizing the Word is like having the fruit tree in your backyard. It is there to nourish you all the time.

Scripture memorization is often considered a dull, burdensome task. But we could get highly motivated if we were given one hundred dollars for every Bible verse we memorized! The rewards of Scripture memory may not always be monetary, but they are a far better treasure for life.

One of the greatest values of Scripture memory is that it keeps us from sin. In Psalm 119:11 NKJV the psalmist wrote: "Your word I have hidden in my heart, That I might not sin against You."

For many people, the morning is the best time to memorize Scripture because their minds are fresh, alert, and free from distractions. There are many different ways to memorize Scripture. Find the one that works best for you, and begin hiding God's Word in your heart so it may bring continual life and nourishment to you. This will produce fruit in your life that you can then share with others.[9]

The bible is God's chart for you to steer
by, to keep you from the bottom of the
sea, and to show you where the harbor is,
and how to reach it without running on
rocks and bars.

HENRY WARD BEECHER

WHOSE WILL?

A Christian woman once confided to a friend that she found it nearly impossible to pray, "Thy will be done." She was afraid of what the Lord might call her to do. Very specifically, she feared being called to a snake- infested swamp to take the Gospel to head-hunting natives. As the mother of a young child, she simply could not bear the thought that God might call her to leave her child and sacrifice her life on the mission field.

> "Not as I will, but as thou wilt."
>
> MATTHEW 26:39 NASB

Her friend said to her, "Suppose your little girl came to you tomorrow morning and said, 'Mommy, I have made up my mind to let you have your own way with me from now on. I'm always going to obey you, and I trust you completely to do everything you think is best for me.' How would you feel?"

The woman replied, "Why, I'd feel wonderful. I'd shower her with hugs and kisses and do everything in my power to give her all the things that were good for her and that would help her find her talents and use them to their fullest."

The friend said, "Well, that's how the Lord feels as your Heavenly Father. His will is going to be far better than anything you have imagined, not far worse."

God's will for Jesus did not end with the pain and suffering of the Cross. The "end" of God's will for Jesus was His glorious resurrection from the dead, His ascension to Heaven, His being seated at the right hand of the Father, and His exaltation as the King of Kings and Lord of Lords forever!

As Hannah Whitall Smith wrote, "Better and sweeter than health, or friends, or money, or fame, or ease, or prosperity, is the adorable will of our God. It gilds the darkest hours with a divine halo, and sheds brightest sunshine on the gloomiest paths . . . it is only a glorious privilege."

Make your prayer today, "Thy will be done, Lord." And then see what good things God has for you to experience!

God is perfect love and perfect wisdom.
We do not pray in order to change his
will, but to bring our wills into harmony
with his.

SIR WILLIAM TEMPLE

PRECIOUS ONES

A young woman named June volunteered at a church agency that served the poor and homeless of her city. One day June met George, who had come in to get some help. Winter was coming, and he needed a jacket and some shoes to help keep him warm. He took a seat in the chapel because the waiting room was crowded and noisy. When he indicated he wanted a Bible, June went to get one for him while he waited his turn in the clothing room. When she returned with a Bible, she sat down to talk with him for a while.

> Since thou wast precious in my sight, thou hast been honourable, and I have loved thee: therefore will I give men for thee, and people for thy life.
>
> ISAIAH 43:4 KJV

George looked like he was in his late fifties or early sixties. His thin hair was beginning to gray. Deep lines marked his face. His hands were stiff, and he had lost part of one finger. It was 1:30 in the afternoon, and he smelled slightly of alcohol. He was a short, slight man, and he spoke softly. He had come into the agency alone, and June wondered if he had any family—or anyone who knew or cared that he existed.

She wrote his name in the front of his Bible along with the date. Then she showed him the study helps in the back that would help him find key passages.

As they talked, the thought occurred to her: *George is one of God's very precious creatures.* She wondered if George knew. She wondered how long it had been since someone had told him. What if he had never been told he was precious to God—and to all God's other children as well?

George had very little influence or stature, but God spoke to June through him that day, saying, "My children need to know they are precious to Me. Please tell them that." Since then she has made that message a part of every encounter she has at the church agency.

Ask the Lord how you might share the message, "You are precious to God," with others today through your words and actions.

Kindness is like a rose, which though
easily crushed and fragile, yet speaks a
language of silent power.

FRANCES J. ROBERTS

THE BIG PICTURE

During World War II, parachutes were constructed by the thousands in factories across the United States. From the worker's point of view, the job was tedious. It required stitching endless lengths of colorless fabric, crouched over a sewing machine eight to ten hours a day. The result of a day's work was a formless, massive heap of cloth that had no visible resemblance to a parachute.

To keep the workers motivated and concerned with quality, the management in one factory held a meeting with its workers each morning. The workers were told approximately how many parachutes had been strapped onto the backs of pilots, copilots, and other "flying" personnel the previous day. They knew just how many men had jumped to safety from disabled planes. The managers encouraged their workers to see the "big picture" of their job.

As a second means of motivation, the workers were asked to form a mental picture of a husband, brother, or son who might be the one saved by the parachute they were sewing.

I go to prepare a place for you. And if I go and prepare a place for you, I will come again, and receive you unto myself; that where I am, there ye may be also.

JOHN 14:2-3 NKJV

The level of quality in that factory was one of the highest on record![10]

Don't let the tedium of each day's chores and responsibilities wear you down so you only see the "stitching" in front of you. Keep your eyes on the big picture. Focus on *why* you do what you do and who will benefit from your work, including those you don't know and may never meet. You may not have all the answers to the question, "Why am I here?" but you can rest assured that the Lord does!

Ultimately, the Bible tells us we will be in Heaven for eternity — and that is the biggest picture of all! God is preparing us for Heaven, just as He is preparing Heaven for us. He is creating us to be the people He wants to live with forever.

Whatever mundane tasks or trivial pursuits you undertake today, see them in the light of eternity. They will take on a whole new meaning!

I would not give one moment of heaven
for all the joys and riches of the world,
even if it lasted for thousands and
thousands of years.

MARTIN LUTHER

WHICH DAY PLANNER?

One of the challenges of our busy lives today is to be organized, so we can "get it all done." There are a number of organizers and calendars available to help us schedule the precious hours of the day. Beepers and mobile telephones give us instant communication with anyone anywhere. We no longer get away from it all because now we can take it all with us!

> The things that I purpose, do I purpose according to the flesh?
>
> 2 CORINTHIANS 1:17 KJV

Sometimes we need to be challenged not to "get it all done," but to slow down and reflect on what it is we are trying to accomplish. We must be sure we are headed in the right direction with our families, our work, our church, our community, and our personal lives.

If we are not careful and prayerful, we may find ourselves agreeing with the modern-day philosopher who noted, "So what if you win the rat race—you are still a rat!"

God has a different "daily planner." The psalmist wrote about it in Psalm 105:

- Give thanks to the Lord.

- Call on His name.

- Make known among the nations what he has done.

- Sing to him, sing praise to him.

- Tell of all his wonderful acts.

- Glory in his holy name.

- Let the hearts of those who seek the Lord rejoice.

- Look to the Lord and his strength.

- Seek his face always.

- Remember the wonders he has done, his miracles, and the judgments he has pronounced.

Each day we have the privilege of consulting with the King of Kings and Lord of Lords to determine what path we will take, what tasks are most important, and who needs us the most.

People who are always in a hurry
seemingly get very little satisfaction out
of life.

MOTTO FROM AN AMISH SCHOOL

EVERY LITTLE BITS HELPS

C an the dead be raised in today's world? It all depends on what has died. Sometimes bringing something to life is simply a matter of hard work and time . . . perhaps even centuries. The staff at Redwood National Park in California will tell you that attempting to do this is definitely worth the effort.

> He who began a good work in you will carry it on to completion.
>
> PHILIPPIANS 1:6

In 1978, the park "grew" by sixty square miles of clear-cut forest. Congress gave the park's managers a challenge: restore the land to its natural state. A warning was also given: the final results of your work won't be visible for hundreds of years.

Work began. Since 1978, roads have been removed, stream and estuary habitats have been repaired, land that was stripped of vegetation has been replanted, and hundreds of haul roads and ski trails have been erased. In the process, the park has become something of a "living laboratory," a means of helping environmental researchers learn more about restoration ecology. What they have learned so far at Redwood has been beneficial to managing the health of other national and state parks.[11]

The next time you think your efforts may be too little too late, remember that the world's tallest tree — located at Redwood — did not grow to be 368 feet high overnight. It takes time to become magnificent.

The Scriptures do not tell us to be restored to our "natural" state, but to be transformed into the image of Christ Jesus. (See Romans 12:2.) This transformation isn't immediate. Some habits and patterns take a long time to change. Hurtful memories require healing and may never be fully erased. New ways of thinking and responding can be slow to develop.

However, our transformation is the work of the Holy Spirit within us, and He never fails! Trust God today to be at work in your transformation—a project that may take all your lifetime and be complete only in eternity, but will end in your eventual wholeness.

To be what we are, and to become what we are capable of becoming, is the only end of life.

ROBERT LOUIS STEVENSON

PERSPECTIVE

E ven though God gives us a brand-new day every twenty-four hours, we seldom begin it with a brand-new outlook. All too often, we regard the day ahead as "just another day." We may see a different date on the calendar, but the day seems filled with the same routine, same troubles, same faces, and same responsibilities.

> I have become all things to all men so that by all possible means I might save some.
>
> 1 CORINTHIANS 9:22

Wouldn't it be wonderful if we could look at each day from a slightly different perspective and, with God's guidance, learn to serve Him better as a result?

A Bible translator named Fraiser learned the importance of different perspectives in a very interesting way. Known simply as "Fraiser of Lisuland" in northern Burma, he translated the Scriptures into the Lisu language. He then went on to do translation work somewhere else for a time, leaving a young fellow with the task of teaching the people to read.

When he returned six months later, he found three students and the teacher seated around a table, the Scriptures open in front of the teacher. Fraiser was amazed to see that as each of the students read for him, he left the Bible where it was—in front of him. The man on the left read it sideways, the man on the right read it sideways but from the other side, and the man across from the teacher read it upside down. Since they had always occupied the same chairs, they each had learned to read from that particular perspective, and they each thought that was how their language was written!

We can be like that too. When we learn something from only one perspective, we may think that it's the only perspective. We have the solution to our problem, but nobody else's. Sometimes it's necessary to change seats and assume a different perspective on the same truth in order to help others.

The principles of truth in God's Word never change, but our understanding of them does! Ask God to give you new insights about Him today. With your new perspective, you may see the solution to a problem that has plagued someone for years.

As our perspective broadens, our ability to help ourselves and others increases.

An investment in knowledge always pay
the best interest.

BENJAMIN FRANKLIN

THE MORNING HOUR

> Be still, and know that I am God; I will be exalted among the nations, I will be exalted in the earth!
>
> PSALM 46:10
> NKJV

So many of us find the morning to be a time of "rushing." Various family members scurry in different directions with different needs and different timetables. One has lost a sock; another can't find last night's homework. One needs a sack lunch; another needs lunch money. One leaves with a kiss; another leaves with a shout; and another needs encouragement to open her eyes as she stumbles out the door.

In sharp contrast stands the age-old advice that we each need a "quiet time" in the morning to center ourselves and to renew our relationship with our Heavenly Father. Carving out that time for yourself may be your supreme challenge of the day, but it is an effort worth its weight in gold, as so aptly stated by Bruce Fogarty:

"THE MORNING HOUR"

Alone with God, in quiet peace,
From earthly cares I find release;
New strength I borrow for each day
As there with God, I stop to pray.

Alone with God, my sins confess'd
He speaks in mercy, I am blest.
I know the kiss of pardon free,
I talk to God, He talks to me.

Alone with God, my vision clears
I see my guilt, the wasted years
I plead for grace to walk His way
And live for Him, from day to day.

Alone with God no sin between
His lovely face so plainly seen;
My guilt all gone, my heart at rest
With Christ, my Lord, my soul is blest.

Lord, keep my life alone for Thee;
From sin and self, Lord, set me free.
And when no more this earth I trod[1]
They'll say, "He walked alone with God."[12]

Fools rush in where angels fear to tread.

ALEXANDER POPE

WHAT ARE YOU DOING TODAY?

I n the Middle Ages a man was sent to a building site in France to see how the workers felt about their labor. He approached the first worker and asked, "What are you doing?"

The worker snapped at him, "Are you blind? I'm cutting these impossible boulders with primitive tools and putting them together the way the boss tells me. I'm sweating under this hot sun. My back is breaking. I'm bored. I make next to nothing!"

The man quickly backed away and found a second worker, to whom he asked the same question: "What are you doing?"

The second worker replied, "I'm shaping these boulders into useable forms. Then they are put together according to the architect's plans. I earn five francs a week, and that supports my wife and family. It's a job. Could be worse."

A little encouraged but not overwhelmed by this response, the man went to yet a third worker. "What are you doing?" he asked.

Praise the Lord, all you Gentiles! Laud Him, all you peoples! For His merciful kindness is great toward us, And the truth of the Lord endures forever.

PSALM 117:1-2 NKJV

"Why, can't you see?" the worker said as he lifted his arm to the sky. "I'm building a cathedral!"[13]

How do you see your work today? Do you see it as drudgery without reward or purpose? Do you see it as "just a job"? Or, do you see your work as part of God's master design?

How we regard our work may not affect whether a task gets done or not. It will, however, have an impact on the quality of our work and our productivity. The real impact of how we feel about a job lies in this: the more positive we feel about our work, the greater the satisfaction we have at day's end and the less damaging stress we internalize. Those who see value in their jobs enjoy a greater sense of purpose.

Any job can be done with grace, dignity, style, and purpose . . . you only have to choose to see it that way!

Reputation is precious, but character is priceless.

UNKNOWN

SOUL SHOWER

Create in me a clean heart, O God.

PSALM 51:10
NKJV

Much of our morning routine is spent getting clean — taking a bath or shower, washing our hair, and brushing our teeth. But how much time and attention do we give to cleaning our hearts? Don't forget to ask God to create a clean heart in you today!

Generous in love — God, give grace!

Huge in mercy — wipe out my bad record.

Scrub away my guilt, soak out my sins in your laundry.

I know how bad I've been; my sins are staring me down.

You're the One I've violated, and you've seen it all, seen the full extent of my evil.

You have all the facts before you; whatever you decide about me is fair.

I've been out of step with you for a long time . . .

What you're after is truth from the inside out.

Enter me, then; conceive a new, true life.

Soak me in your laundry and I'll come out clean, scrub me and I'll have a snow-white life.

Tune me in to foot-tapping songs, set these once-broken bones to dancing.

Don't look too close for blemishes, give me a clean bill of health.

God, make a fresh start in me, shape a Genesis week from the chaos of my life.

Don't throw me out with the trash, or fail to breathe holiness in me.

Bring me back from gray exile, put a fresh wind in my sails!

Give me a job teaching rebels your ways so the lost can find their way home.

Commute my death sentence, God, my salvation God, and I'll sing anthems to your life-giving ways.

Unbutton my lips, dear God; I'll let loose with your praise.

PSALM 51, MSG[14]

Clean hands, clean heart

Help me, Lord, to do my part.

ROBERTA S. CULLEY

RECIPROCITY

Sometimes when we focus on helping others, we end up solving our own problems. That certainly was true for David, an eight-year-old from Wisconsin who had a speech impediment. His problem made him hesitant to read aloud or speak up in class.

David's mother also had a problem—multiple sclerosis. One winter day she and David were out walking, and her cane slipped on an icy patch, causing her to fall. She was unhurt, but the incident left David wishing he could do something to help her.

Some time later, David's teacher assigned her students to come up with an invention for a national contest. He decided he would invent a cane that wouldn't slide on ice by putting a nail on the bottom of it. After his mother expressed concern about the nail damaging floor coverings, he developed a retractable system. Much like a ballpoint pen, the nail could be popped out of sight by releasing a button at the top of the cane.

> Pray for each other so that you may be healed.
>
> JAMES 5:16

David's invention earned him first prize in the contest. As the winner, he was required to make public appearances and communicate with those who expressed an interest in his project. The more he talked about the cane, the less noticeable his speech impediment became![15]

Who needs your help today?

They may not need you to invent something for them. They may simply need your assistance on a project, a word of encouragement, or prayer for a particular problem. You will find, as you extend the effort, time, and energy to help someone, that something inside you will be softened, healed, renewed, or strengthened. An outward expression toward others always does something inwardly that enables, empowers, and enhances the character of Christ Jesus in us.

That's God's principle of reciprocity!

Little deeds of kindness, little words of love,
Help make earth happy like the heaven above.

JULIA FLETCHER CARNEY

FORGIVENESS

One morning Denise Stovall's daughter, Deanna, taught her a special lesson about forgiveness. "Mama! How do you spell Louis?" Deanna asked as she rushed into the kitchen.

"Louis? Who's Louis?" asked Denise.

"You know," said the five-year-old. "He's the boy who gave me my black eye."

> "Forgive us our debts, as we also have forgiven our debtors."
>
> MATTHEW 6:12

For several days Denise had asked herself how a child could be so mean to another child. Anger sizzled inside her every time she saw the black and blue mark around Deanna's bright hazel eye. "Why on earth do you want to know how to spell his name—especially after what he did to you?"

Deanna's reply reminded Denise of why Jesus said, "Let the little children come unto me, for of such is the kingdom of Heaven."

"W-e-l-l, at church yesterday, Miss Mae told us we should make paper chains for All Saints Day. She said to make a ring every time somebody does a nice thing like Jesus did, and then put that person's name on the ring. Louis told me on the bus today that he was sorry he hit me in my eye, and that was nice. I want to put his name on this ring and make it part of the chain, so we can pray for him so he won't do it again."

As Denise stood in the middle of the kitchen with her hands on her hips, the words of a recent sermon came back to convict her: "Forgiveness, no matter how long it takes or how difficult it is to attain, is the only path to healing and freedom."

Upon reflection, Denise thought Deanna's bruised eyelid looked just a *little* better.[16]

Before you start the day, make certain you are free from all unforgiveness and offense. Remember how much God has forgiven you, and it will be easier to forgive others!

Forgiveness is the attribute of the strong.

The weak can never forgive.

MAHATMA GANDHI

INVITED TO BREAKFAST

Most people wake up to an alarm clock ringing at an appointed hour rather than to a rooster crowing in the barnyard. But for the Apostle Peter, the crowing rooster on the early morning of Jesus' crucifixion was a "wake-up call"—it woke him up to who he really was. In Peter's worst moment he had denied knowing his Friend and Teacher, Jesus. He wept bitterly over his betrayal and must have felt terrible guilt and shame afterward.

> You, O Lord
> . . . know
> the hearts
> of all.
>
> ACTS 1:24 NKJV

Then one morning after His resurrection, Jesus appeared to the disciples, who were fishing at the Sea of Tiberias. He called out from the shore and asked if they had caught any fish. The disciples didn't recognize Him and called back no. Jesus told them to throw the net on the other side of the boat, and the catch was so great they were unable to haul it in. Now they knew the Man directing them was Jesus, and they headed to shore.

When the disciples got there, Jesus invited them to eat with Him. "Come and have breakfast," He said. In the dawning hours of the day, the resurrected Jesus cooked breakfast for them.

How do you think Peter felt when, after the greatest failure of his life, Jesus wanted to spend time with him, eat with him, and even help him fish? Jesus sought out the disciple who had let Him down when He needed him most. Moreover, He called Peter to lead His followers.

Like Peter, there are experiences in our days that serve as "wake-up calls" to who we claim to be. Those "wake-up calls" come in the form of opportunities to compromise who we are and what we believe. How do we act when others aren't around? How do we handle situations that can violate our integrity? To live a compromised life is to deny Jesus—the same as Peter did. (See Titus 1:16.)

It is always important for us to spend time with the Lord, but when we need to come clean in our heart, it is especially important. Jesus always invites us to fellowship with Him; He always forgives.

Whatever mistakes or compromises we made yesterday, Jesus still loves us today and says, "Come and have breakfast with Me."

Whether we stumble or whether we fall,
we must only think of rising again and
going on in our course.

FRANÇOIS FÉNELON

THE VALUE OF ONE

Some days it's hard just to get out of bed. Our motivation is either fading, or it's completely gone. We are overcome with a "What difference does it make?" attitude. We become overwhelmed at the complexity of the duties before us. Our talents and resources seem minuscule in comparison to the task.

"There is joy in the presence of the angels of God over one sinner who repents."

LUKE 15:10 NASB

A businessman and his wife once took a much-needed getaway at an oceanside hotel. During their stay a powerful storm arose, lashing the beach and sending massive breakers against the shore. The storm woke the man. He lay still in bed listening to the storm's fury and reflecting on his own life of constant and continual demands and pressures.

Before daybreak the wind subsided. The man got out of bed to go outside and survey the damage done by the storm. He walked along the beach and noticed it was covered with starfish that had been thrown ashore by the massive waves. They laid helpless on the sandy beach. Unable to get to the water, the starfish faced inevitable death as the sun's rays dried them out.

Farther down the beach, the man saw a figure walking along the shore. Every once in a while, the figure would stoop and pick something up. In the dim of the early-morning twilight, he couldn't quite make it all out.

As he approached, he realized it was a young boy picking up the starfish one at a time and flinging them back into the ocean to safety.

As the man neared the young boy, he said, "Why are you doing that? One person will never make a difference — there are too many starfish to get back into the water before the sun comes up."

The boy said sadly, "Yes, that's true" and then bent to pick up another starfish. Then he said, "But I can sure make a difference to that one."

God never intended for an individual to solve all of life's problems. But He did intend for each one of us to use whatever resources and gifts He gave us to make a difference where we are.[17]

Those who bring sunshine to the lives of
others cannot keep it from themselves.

SIR JAMES M. BARRIE

WHO SAYS YOU CAN'T?

You can do anything. That's what Kent Cullers's parents told him as he was growing up. That's what many parents tell their children. But Cullers was born blind. Even so, if a child hears the phrase, *You can do anything,* often enough, it eventually sinks in. It bears fruit. And it certainly did in Cullers's case.

As a young boy, he insisted on climbing trees and riding a bicycle. His father arranged a job transfer to California so the boy could attend a regular school, and Cullers became a straight-A student. He was valedictorian of his high-school class and a National Merit Scholar. He went on to earn a Ph.D. in physics.

> I can do all things through Christ who strengthens me.
>
> PHILIPPIANS 4:13 NKJV

Cullers's first love has always been space, so it seems fitting that he found himself employed at NASA. As a researcher, one of his jobs is to design equipment to help scientists search for signs of intelligent communication in outer space.[18]

How does this blind man see what others can't? He uses his "mind's eye." He also uses his other senses—perhaps a little better than most people. Above all, he continues to tell himself what his parents taught him early in life: You can do anything.

The Apostle Paul would have added a key phrase to

Cullers's parental advice: *through Christ who gives me strength.* The Source of all our ability, energy, and creativity is the Lord himself. It is He who challenges us to go forward and equips us to get the task done. It is the Lord working in us to enable us, working through us to empower us, and working on our behalf to enrich us.

At the same time, the Lord expects us to do two things: first, to open ourselves to His presence and power; and second, to get in gear. He calls us to believe and to do.

What are you believing today? What are you doing? Activate both your believing and doing; synchronize both with the will of God; and you can't help but be launched to a higher and better position.

If you think you can or can't do
something . . . you're probably right.

HENRY FORD

PROCRASTINATION LEADS NOWHERE

I will hasten
and not
delay to
obey your
commands.

PSALM 119:60

Morning is a great time to make a list of things to do and plan the day. It's also the best time to tackle those tasks that are the most difficult or least enjoyable. If we procrastinate as the day wears on, rationalization sets in, and sometimes even the tasks we had considered to be the most important are left undone.

Here's a little poem just for those who struggle with procrastination:

"HOW AND WHEN"

We are often greatly bothered
By two fussy little men,
Who sometimes block our pathway
Their names are How and When.
If we have a task or duty
Which we can put off a while,
And we do not go and do it
You should see those two rogues smile!
But there is a way to beat them,
And I will tell you how:
If you have a task or duty,
Do it well, and do it now.

UNKNOWN

As part of your morning prayer time, ask the Lord to help you to overcome any tendency to procrastinate and instead to prioritize projects according to His plans and purposes.

Often we ask the Lord, "What do You want me to do?" but then fail to ask Him one of the key follow-up questions: "When do You want me to do this?" When we have a sense of God's timing, and in some cases His urgency about a matter, our conviction grows to get the job done right away.

God's omnipresence means He is always with you, and He is always timely. He's with you in the "now" moments of your life. He is concerned with how you use every moment of your time. Recognize that He desires to be part of your time-management and task-completion process today!

Never leave till tomorrow that which you
can do today.

BENJAMIN FRANKLIN

A CORK'S INFLUENCE

A tour group passed through a particular room in a factory. They viewed an elongated bar of steel, which weighed five hundred pounds, suspended vertically by a chain. Near it, an average-sized cork was suspended by a silk thread.

"You will see something shortly which is seemingly impossible," said an attendant to the group of sightseers. "This cork is going to set this steel bar in motion!"

> Let us behave decently, as in the daytime . . . clothe yourselves with the Lord Jesus Christ.
>
> ROMANS 13:13-14

She took the cork in her hand, pulled it only slightly to the side of its original position, and released it. The cork swung gently against the steel bar, which remained motionless.

For ten minutes the cork, with pendulum-like regularity, struck the iron bar. Finally, the bar vibrated slightly. By the time the tour group passed through the room an hour later, the great bar was swinging like the pendulum of a clock!

Many of us feel we are not exerting a feather's weight of influence upon others or making a dent in the bastions of evil in the world. Not so! Other people can be powerfully impacted when they see us walking in God's goodness.

Not everyone is called to spread the love of Jesus through the pulpit, on the evangelistic trail, or in a full-time counseling ministry. Most of us are called to live our lives as "corks," through word and example — quietly, gently tapping away through the work of our daily lives. Tap by loving tap, in God's time, even the quietest Christian can make a huge difference in the lives of those whom preachers may never reach.

One modern-day philosopher has estimated that the average person encounters at least twenty different people in the course of a day, with a minimum of eye contact and exchange of words or gestures. That's at least twenty opportunities for a cork to "tap" at human hearts.

As you go about your day, remember that even a smile can warm strangers' hearts and draw them to Jesus.

Wear a smile and have friends; wear a
scowl and have wrinkles.

GEORGE ELIOT

STAYING CHARGED UP

The age we live in has been described as the age of the to-do list that can't be done. Facing overwhelming demands, we find it hard to give ourselves permission to rest or take a break. But the rewards — renewed perspective, clearer insight, physical energy, and spiritual preparedness — are well worth it.

> Let the people renew their strength.
>
> ISAIAH 41:1 KJV

Before automatic headlight controls were installed in automobiles, it was easy to park a car and leave the headlights on. Perhaps we were in a hurry, or it was light enough outside that we forgot we had turned the lights on. If we were gone for very long, we returned to find the car battery dead. To get the car running again, the battery had to be recharged.

Just like a car battery, our own supply of energy is not infinite. We must replenish it frequently with sleep, rest, food, and relaxation. Our busy nonstop days can be draining. Operating at top speed, we utilize all available emotional, physical, mental, and spiritual resources. Before we know it, our energy is consumed.

Unless we pay careful attention, we will drain our "battery" to the point of feeling "dead on our feet." Being fatigued can cause our perception to be distorted and our responses to others to be negative. Furthermore, if we fail to do something about it, over time it can result in physical or emotional illness.

Charles Spurgeon, a well-known nineteenth-century preacher once said, "Without constant restoration we are not ready for the perpetual assaults. If we allow the good in our lives to get weak — or our 'light' to grow dim — the evil will surely gather strength and struggle desperately for the mastery over us."

You are wise to take a short break now and then during the day. Living this way will help you to maintain your energy supply and enable you to be more productive and content.

If you are swept off your feet, it's time to get on your knees.

FRED BECK

WITH ATTITUDE

"To love what you do and feel that it matters—how could anything be more fun?" asks Katharine Graham. That's what we all desire, isn't it?

> Whatever you do, do all to the glory of God.
>
> 1 CORINTHIANS 10:31 RSV

No matter what work we do, our attitude toward our work is vital to our basic sense of self-worth. The ideal for everyone is to love the work they do and feel that it has significance. While no job is enjoyable or pleasant all the time, it is possible to derive satisfaction from what we bring to a job—the attitude with which we perform our tasks.

For example, Brother Lawrence, the seventeenth-century Carmelite, found joy in his job washing dishes at the monastery. In the monotony of his routine work, he found the opportunity to focus on God and feel His presence.

Modern-day entrepreneurs Ben Cohen and Jerry Greenfield make and sell ice cream with a purpose. The bottom line of Ben & Jerry's Homemade, Inc., is "How much money is left over at the end of the year?" and "How have we improved life in the community?"

"Leftover money" goes to fund Ben & Jerry's Foundation, which distributes funds to worthy nonprofit causes. These are charities that help needy children, preserve the Amazonian rain forest, provide safe shelter for emotionally or psychologically distressed people, and fund a business staffed by unemployed homeless people. By helping others with their profits, Ben and Jerry put more meaning into their ice cream business.

The Scriptures teach that all service ranks the same with God because it is not what you do that matters, but the spirit in which you do it. Street sweepers who does their work to serve God and bless the people who travel on the streets are as pleasing to Him as the priests or pastors who teach and nurture their congregations.

If you feel your work is insignificant, ask God to open your eyes! When you do all for Him and to serve others, no task is unimportant!

People who make room in their hearts for
others will themselves find
accommodation everywhere.

UNKNOWN

DAY BY DAY

A mother once stopped by her recently married daughter's home unexpectedly and was promptly greeted with a flood of tears. Alarmed, the mother asked, "What happened, dear?"

> "Give us this day our daily bread."
>
> MATTHEW 6:11 KJV

Her daughter replied, "It's not what happened, but what keeps happening!"

Even more concerned, the mother asked, "What is it that keeps happening?"

The daughter replied, "Every day there are dishes to be washed. Every day there are meals to be prepared and a lunch to be packed. Every day there is laundry to be done and beds to be made and a house to be cleaned."

"And?" the mother asked, still unsure as to the nature of the problem.

"Don't you see?" the daughter said through her tears. "Life is just so daily."

On those days when the "daily-ness" of life seems to have you bogged down in boredom or drudgery, remind yourself the Lord said He would provide for the needs of His people on a daily basis. Manna was gathered in the wilderness every morning. Jesus taught His disciples to pray for their "daily bread." God wants to provide what we need, not only physically and materially, but also emotionally and spiritually, one day at a time.

• Trust the Lord to give to you

• material goods, money, food, and supplies that you will need today.

• ideas and creative energy that you need for today's work.

• stamina, health, and strength that you need today to fulfill your many roles and responsibilities.

• spiritual nourishment and fortitude to face and conquer the temptations and trials of today.

The Lord is with you all day, every day, day by day!

God gives us the ingredients for our daily bread, but he expects us to do the baking.

UNKNOWN

A QUIET MOMENT

Between the great issues of life there is quiet. Silence characterizes the highest in art and the deepest in nature. It's the silence between the notes that give them rhythm, interest, and emphasis.

The surest spiritual search is made in silence. Moses learned in Midian and Paul in Arabia what would have eluded them in the noisy streets of men.

Silence reaches beyond words. The highest point in drama is silence. The strongest of emotions don't always cry aloud. The most effective reproof is not a tongue lashing. The sincerest sympathy is not wordy or noisy. The best preparation for an emergency is the calm of quietness.

> For thus saith the Lord God, the Holy One of Israel; In returning and rest shall ye be saved; in quietness and in confidence shall be your strength . . .
>
> ISAIAH 30:15 KJV

Time spent in quiet prayer is the best preparation for intelligent action. The best proof of quality is often silence; the great engine is almost noiseless. The best indicator of confidence is almost always silence; people who are confident of their position do not argue or raise their voices or even try to explain everything.

Quiet times are most cherished in the middle of busy days. Sometimes the quiet does not offer itself; it must be sought out. At other times, the surroundings don't allow for true silence. It is in those moments when the Holy Spirit can supernaturally turn down the volume and allow moments of quiet communion with God from within.

A coffee break is a perfect time to seek a quiet spot for a few minutes of real refreshment in the presence of a "still small voice" (1 Kings 19:12 KJV).

Silence is a great peacemaker.

HENRY WADSWORTH LONGFELLOW

A KITE'S TALE

During the Sunday children's sermon, a pastor gathered the little ones around him and told this story:

> Just as each of us has one body with many members, and these members do not all have the same function.
>
> ROMANS 12:4

On a breezy March day, the town mayor happened through the park where a small boy was flying the largest, most beautiful kite he had ever seen. It soared so high and floated so gently, the mayor was sure it must be visible from the next town. Since his little town did not have very many things of note to its credit, the mayor decided to award a "key to the city" to the one responsible for setting this spectacle aloft.

"Who is responsible for flying this kite?" the mayor inquired.

"I am," said the boy. "I made the kite with my own hands. I painted all the beautiful pictures and constructed it with scraps I found in my father's workshop. I fly the kite," he declared.

"I am," said the wind. "It is my whim that keeps it aloft and sets the direction it will go. Unless I blow, the kite will not fly at all. I fly the kite," the wind cooed.

"Not so," exclaimed the kite's tail. "I make it sail and give it stability against the wind's whims. Without me, the kite would spin out of control and not even the boy could save it from crashing to earth. I fly the kite," declared the tail.

"Now who flies the kite?" the pastor asked the children.

"They all do!" said several kids in concert. Smart kids!

Sometimes adults aren't so smart. In the hurry of a business day, it's easy to forget that the boss or team leader is just that, the leader of the team. Each member is important in keeping projects moving and meeting goals.

Take a moment to consider your coworkers. Ask yourself, *How would our progress be changed if that person's job didn't exist?* Next time you pass their work area, tell them you're glad they are part of the team.

───────────────

Kind words don't wear out the tongue.

CHINESE PROVERB

THE EMPTY TOMB

P hilip was born with Down's syndrome. He was a happy child, but as he grew older he became increasingly aware that he was different from other children.

He went to Sunday school with boys and girls his own age, and the class had wonderful experiences together — learning, laughing, playing. But Philip remained an outsider.

As an Easter lesson, the Sunday school teacher gave each student a large egg-shaped plastic container. The children were asked to explore the church grounds, find something that symbolized new life to them, put it in their "egg," and bring it back to share with the class.

The children had a grand time running about the churchyard collecting symbols. Then they gathered back in the classroom, put their eggs on the table, and watched with great anticipation as the teacher opened each egg. In one egg, there was a flower, in another a butterfly. The students responded with great glee and enthusiasm as the teacher revealed the contents of each egg . . . a branch, a leaf, a flower bud.

When the teacher opened the next egg, there was nothing in it. As could be expected, the eight-year-olds responded, "That's not fair — that's stupid! Somebody didn't do it right."

Philip went up to the teacher, tugged on her sleeve, and said, "It's mine. That egg is mine."

The children laughed and said, "You never do anything right, Philip. There's nothing there."

Philip replied, "I did so do it. I did do it. It's empty — the tomb is empty!"

The classroom fell silent. From that day on things were different. Philip became a full-fledged part of the class. The children took him into their friendship. He had been freed from the tomb of his being different, and he entered in to a new life among his peers.[19]

You must look into people,

as well as at them.

LORD CHESTERFIELD

GIVE ME A WORD

Marjorie Holmes writes in *Lord, Let Me Love* about her daughter, who had a fascination with words at a young age. From her earliest attempts at talking, she liked to try out new words and sounds. Often she would chant and sing words or make up strange combinations of sounds to build her own vocabulary.

> The word was God.
>
> JOHN 1:1 NKJV

She was impatient, however, because all the things she was learning far exceeded her ability to express them. Because she needed more words, she began asking her mother for words, just as she might ask her for a cookie or a hug.

The little girl would ask, "Give me a bright word, Mother." Marjorie would answer with a string of nouns and adjectives that described the word bright, such as "sunshine, golden, luminous, shiny, and sparkling."

Then she would ask for a soft word. Marjorie responded, "Velvety soft like a blackberry or a pony's nose. Or furry, like your kitten. Or how about a lullaby?" And when her daughter was angry, she would demand a glad word. The game continued until the little girl's attitude was transformed by the happy thoughts prompted by happy words.[20]

Through words, God spoke creation into being. He said, "Let there be light." And there was light. He said, "Let us make the earth and the fullness of it." And foliage, animals, birds, and fish were created.

God gave us His Word so we could live full and satisfying lives while we are here on earth. The Bible is teeming with wonderful, powerful, beautiful words for our daily lives.

What word do you need today? Do you need a glad word or a comforting word? "Give me a word," can be the prayer of your heart to God during your coffee break — then open your Bible and let Him speak!

Try these: a kind thought—a kind word—and a good deed.

ELBERT HUBBARD

A TIME TO PRAY

Several years ago a television ad focused on a lovely young woman's smiling face. She was looking down and obviously very busy at the task before her, although what she was doing was not shown. At the same time she was busy with this task, she was praying. The ad's emphasis was on taking time to pray no matter what else we must do during the day.

As the camera moved away from this young woman's face and down to what she was doing, it became clear that this was a young mother diapering her baby.

> He has made everything appropriate in its time.
>
> ECCLESIASTES
> 3:11 NASB

What a lovely picture of how easy it is for us to talk with the Lord! Setting a chunk of time aside every morning might not work every day for you, but during each twenty-four-hour day you can creatively find a portion of time that is just for God.

We mutter and sputter,
We fume and we spurt,
We mumble and grumble,
Our feelings get hurt.
We can't understand things,
Our vision grows dim,
When all that we need is:
A moment with Him.[21]

UNKNOWN

Most of us are so busy during the day that we find it increasingly difficult to set aside a block of time to spend in prayer, not just a quick prayer of thanks, but a time of genuine communication with the Lord.

God wants this time with us, and we need it with Him. There are times we can be alone with the Savior, but we need to creatively look for them.

I cannot be the man I should be without times of quietness. Stillness is an essential part of growing deeper.

CHARLES R. SWINDOLL

MORE THAN ATOMS

Two young brothers were engaged in their on-going battle for sibling superiority. Adam, age nine, was explaining to four-year-old Rob the science of living matter, taking no small pleasure in his advantage of a third grade education.

Soon, a skirmish broke loose, with cries of "Am not!" and "Are too!!" ringing through the house. Rob ran crying to find his mother.

> But let each one examine his own work, and then he will have rejoicing in himself alone, and not in another.
>
> GALATIANS 6:4
> NKJV

"Mo-o-o-m . . . is everything made of atoms?"

"Yes, that's true."

"But," he said, "I'm made of atoms!"

"Sweetie, he's right. Everything in the world is made of atoms."

Rob sank to the floor, sobbing as if his heart had broken. His perplexed mom picked him up, hugged him, and asked, "What on earth is the matter?"

"It's no fair!" he howled. "I don't want to be made of Adams—I want to be made of *Robs*!!"

We all want recognition for our "specialness." But we should never strive to gain our self-worth from our society, feedback from others, or our own comparisons to others. Our self-esteem should be based in the fact that God created us with the utmost care and has called His creation good.[22]

In His foresight we are all made of "the right stuff." Our self-worth then comes from how we use it — serving our families and communities, exercising our creative gifts, and becoming one with God. No amount of stature in the eyes of people can equal the reward of following God's will. That's how we grow into more than just a collection of atoms!

Self-esteem is a fragile flower and can be
crushed so easily.

JAMES C. DOBSON

OBEDIENCE AND PEACEFUL ABIDING

W hile on safari, a missionary family stopped for lunch. The children were playing under a tree a distance away from their parents and the other adults on the team. Suddenly the father of one child jumped up and yelled to his son, "Drop down!" and the son did so instantly. Others in the group were shocked to learn that a poisonous snake was slithering down the tree ready to strike the child. It would have meant certain death if the snake had bitten him. Only the father of the child saw the snake.

"Abide in me, and I in you."

JOHN 15:4
NASB

Amazement was expressed over the instant response of the child to his father's command. The father explained that the abiding love he and his son enjoyed had developed from the trust they had in each other. The boy did not question when his dad gave the command; he trusted him and responded accordingly. The missionary father also expected his son to respond to his command.

The peaceful rest that both of them were able to enjoy later that day was evidence of the abiding rest that God has for each of us as we learn to trust Him. Are you abiding in Christ?

God wants to abide in us, and He wants us to abide in Him. Abiding comes more easily for some than others. It is not always easy to know what God has planned for us, but we can be assured that whatever it is, He is ready to equip us with what we need to endure and hold on to that place for as long as He wants us there. Abiding starts with trust and ends with complete rest.

———————————————

All I have seen teaches me to trust the creator for all I have not seen.

RALPH WALDO EMERSON

BUT WHEN?

We have often smiled knowingly at that kitchen-magnet quip, "Lord, give me patience, and give it to me now!" And why not? Our society expects immediate accomplishment in almost everything we do—from microwave meals in minutes to global communication in seconds.

It seems, whatever the problem, there should be a button, switch, or pill to deliver fast results. This makes it all the more difficult to accept that, like it or not, spiritual growth takes time.

> Wait on the Lord; be of good courage, and he shall strengthen your heart.
>
> PSALM 27:14
> NKJV

In a garden, all seedlings have average schedules of development. But as human beings with unique histories and needs, we can't rely on averages to determine when we might take that next step in our walk with God.

It's tempting, when faced with a flaw of the spirit or other growth issue, to pray for and expect immediate change. Sometimes it happens. But how lost and confused we feel if our prayers don't bring the instant relief we seek!

During such times, it's good to remember that all facets of our nature—whether traits we love about ourselves or those we want to improve—are part of our God-created being. Even our less-than-desirable parts are there for a reason and contain His lessons for us.

When change seems to come slowly, don't give up hope. Consider that the timetable for your growth is in the Lord's hands. Continue your daily communion with God and trust your spirit to be healed in His time.

———————————————————

He that can have patience can have what he wills.

BENJAMIN FRANKLIN

MORNING THIRST

T he need for a refreshing drink when we first wake in the morning is often so strong that we find ourselves anticipating the taste before we ever get a glass in our hands. That thirst is a driving force that nothing else will satisfy.

> My soul thirsts for God, for the living God.
>
> PSALM 42:2 NASB

There is another thirst that needs to be quenched when we first wake up. It is a thirst we often ignore until it is so great, everything else in our lives—our relationships, our growth as children of God, our joy, our peace—begins to wither.

Patti did not have running water inside her home when she was a child. Not since then has she known that same level of satisfaction a morning drink of water can give. This was especially true if the water in the house ran out during the night when it was too cold or too stormy for anyone to make a trip to the source outside. Sometimes it was a long, long wait for morning.

There is a source of living water that is available to us any time of the day or night. It never runs out, it never gets contaminated, it never freezes over, and it is always as refreshing throughout the day as it was with the first sip in the morning.

Renowned missionary Hudson Taylor once said, "There is a living God, He has spoken in the Bible and He means what He says and He will do all that He has promised." He has promised to quench our thirst in such a way that we will never be thirsty again!

Are you anticipating a drink from God's cup of refreshing living water in the morning? God gives you permission to start sipping right now. Bon Appetit!

When you drink from the stream,

remember the spring.

CHINESE PROVERB

THE FACE OF GOD

Dutch psychologist and theologian Henri Nouwen was known for his determination to break down barriers, whether between Catholic and Protestant or therapist and patient. He spent most of his life pursuing a high-pressure career as a sought-after speaker and author.

But years of travel and dozens of books took such a toll on his health and spirit that he eventually retreated to Toronto, Canada, to become priest-in-residence at Daybreak, a home for the severely disabled.

Nouwen lived a quiet life at Daybreak, residing in a small, simple room and ministering to the patients at the facility. He had a special relationship with a resident named Adam, a profoundly retarded young man unable to walk, talk, or care for himself. Nouwen devoted nearly two hours every day to caring for Adam—bathing, shaving, combing his hair, and feeding him.

To onlookers, it seemed a great burden on the priest to spend so many hours on such menial duties. But when asked why he spent his time in this way, Nouwen insisted that it was he who benefited from the relationship. He described how the process of learning to love Adam,

No one has ever seen God; if we love one another, God remains in us, and His love is perfected in us.

1 JOHN 4:12 NASB

with all of his incapacities, taught him what it must be like for God to love us, even with all our frailties.

Ultimately, Henri Nouwen concluded that "the goal of education and formation for the ministry is continually to recognize the Lord's voice, His face, and His touch in every person we meet."[23]

Have you seen the Lord's face lately?

There is no remedy for love than to love more.

HENRY DAVID THOREAU

WHAT DO YOU THINK?

"**D**ad, have you heard of this book?" Cindy asked, showing him a copy of a highly controversial work. Rev. Bill looked up from his desk to respond to his sixteen-year-old daughter.

"Sure, I have. Why do you ask?" he replied.

The eyes of the Lord preserve knowledge.

PROVERBS 22:12 KJV

In fact, he knew a great deal about the book. It had recently been made into a movie that was causing quite a stir in the Christian community, and many pastors and church members were so upset that they had even picketed the theaters where the movie was showing.

"I was just wondering if it's a good book," Cindy answered.

"Why don't you read it for yourself, and then we will talk about it together," he suggested.

In that moment, Bill demonstrated a remarkable faith in his daughter, his own parenting, and his God. By inviting her to read and discuss this book, he showed that he trusted Cindy to think for herself. Beyond his faith in her, he modeled his faith in God by trusting that He would provide guidance as she made decisions.

The single greatest challenge we face as parents is that of letting go of our children in the right way and at the right time. Nowhere is this faith challenged more than in the arena of controversial ideas. Yet, we can have confidence that what we have taught them will keep them, for Scripture says, "Train a child in the way he should go, and when he is old he will not turn from it" (Proverbs 22:6).

Bill could trust Cindy because he knew that her entire life had been one characterized by learning the Word of God, and now it was time to put that learning to the test.

———————————————

While yielding to loving parental leaderships, children are also learning to yield to the benevolent leadership of God himself.

JAMES C. DOBSON

TOUCHING LIFE

> Preserve
> my life
> accordingly
> to your
> love.
>
> PSALM 119:88

The sounds of the delivery room receded to a quiet murmur of post-delivery activities and near-whispered comments between the parents. The father, gowned, with a hair net and masked face, leaned forward and touched their child who was cuddled to the mother. She looked down on the baby who was scowling, eyes tightly shut. With a sense of awe, the mother stretched forth one finger to gently smooth the child's wrinkled forehead. The need to touch her daughter was urgent, yet she was careful.

Developmental psychologists who have examined the process of childbirth and witnessed thousands of deliveries inform us that the need to gently touch one's newborn is a near-universal impulse crossing all cultural boundaries. Obviously, we have been created with an innate need to physically connect with our offspring. In this sense we are very much like God.

In *The Creation of Adam,* one of Michelangelo's famous frescoes that decorate the ceiling of the Sistine Chapel, he portrays the hand of Adam outstretched with a finger pointed. Opposite to it you see the hand of God in a similar pose reaching toward man. The two fingertips are nearly touching. No image more clearly reveals the Father's heart. He is ever-reaching out His hand to touch, with gentleness and love, those who are created in His own image.

Mothers and God share a common bond then, do they not? Both possess a deep reverence for the life that they have brought into the world. Both yearn to touch those made in their image.

The love of a mother is the veil of a softer light between the heart and the heavenly Father.

SAMUEL TAYLOR COLERIDGE

SUNRISE

S unrise, shining its beams through the window on a cold winter's morning, is a welcome sight. Even if the air outside is icy cold, sunrise gives the illusion of warmth. With the rising sun, the city opens its shutters and makes preparations for the day; in the country, the farm animals are let out to pasture. Kids are off to school, adults are on their way to work, and each has a different perspective of the sunrise.

Sunrise happens whether we see it or not. Clouds may cover the sky so totally that we can't experience the beauty of the sunbeams making their way to the earth. No matter what the climate, the sun still rises in the eastern horizon and sets over the west. Sunrise is set by God's clock, and it is ours to enjoy in the early mornings when we can see it clearly. It is just as much there for us to enjoy when the cloud shadows cover it. We can trust it to be there — even though it may be hidden for a while.

We can also trust God to be there every morning because He is the one, irrefutable Reality in this life, and He remains constant and true!

The sunrise from on high shall visit us.

LUKE 1:78 NASB

Life is a mixture of sunshine and rain,

Laughter and teardrops,

Please and pain—

Low tides and high tides,

Mountains and plains,

Triumphs, defeats, and losses and gains,

But there never was a cloud

That the Son didn't shine through

And there's nothing that's impossible

For Jesus Christ to do!

HELEN STEINER RICE

I KNOW THAT VOICE!

A young mother had been alone with her preschoolers for a week while her husband was away on a business trip. The fourth day was particularly exasperating. After several bedtime stories, she finally got the energetic children to bed and decided to relax. She had changed into an old pair of sweats and shampooed her hair when she heard the children jumping around in their room.

> "The sheep follow him because they know his voice."
>
> JOHN 10:4
> NASB

Wrapping a towel around her head, she went to scold them. As she walked out of the children's room, she overheard the littlest one ask, "Who was that?"

In our busy lives we often overlook God's presence. We can be so out of practice at listening to Him that we fail to recognize His voice, and then we miss out on His guidance and grace. Have you ever found yourself asking, "Who was that?" only later to realize that it was indeed Christ?

When a sheep refuses to follow, the shepherd has no choice but to teach the sheep a lesson for its own protection. The shepherd will break one of the sheep's legs and carry the sheep around his neck until its leg heals. The animal becomes so acquainted with its master's voice and ways that it then graciously follows and obeys. Though a difficult lesson, the shepherd saves one who would otherwise be lost.

God wants us to know Him so well that we immediately recognize His voice and obey His commands. There is no better way to know the Master's voice than through an intimate relationship with Him. A perfect time to develop an awareness of the Father's voice is in the early morning when we can quietly sit and listen.

If you keep watch over your hearts, and
listen for the voice of God and learn of
Him, in one short hour you can learn
more from Him than you could learn from
man in a thousand years.

JOHANN TAULER

WHAT SHOULD WE DO?

> "The King will reply, 'Truly I tell you, whatever you did for one of the least of these brothers and sisters of mine, you did for me.'"
>
> MATTHEW 25:40

You see them on the streets of every major city — the homeless. They live in a culture of their own in modern America, existing day-to-day in a world of hand-outs and hand-me-downs. Their presence is a source of heated debates in many cities, and no one seems to want them in "my neighborhood."

Where do they come from, and what should be done about them?

One answer can be found in the life of P. W. Alexander and her essay "Christmas at Home," where she reflects on her dedication to community service — much of which involves caring for the homeless. She writes, "As a child I did not look forward to the holidays. It began with Halloween. In the morning we went to church and in the evening we collected for UNICEF. Thanksgiving and Christmas were equally painful. My mother would sign us all up to work at the soup kitchen."[24]

Thus, she was raised in the art of serving, and as she grew older she began to understand better the reasons why her mother insisted that they care for others during the holidays. In fact, the closing words of her essay demonstrate the impact of her mother's actions: "I do this not out of a sense of duty or obligation; I do it because it is my family tradition."[25]

What neat family traditions are you creating for your children?

Dedicate some of your life to others. Your dedication will not be a sacrifice; it will be an exhilarating experience.

THOMAS DOOLEY

THE BIRTHDAY SURPRISE

I t was one of those dreadful evenings every family experiences on occasion. Though it was Saturday night—and a pre-birthday celebration at that—nothing was going right. Even the ride home from the restaurant was lousy.

> Let all that you do be done with love.
>
> 1 CORINTHIANS 16:14 NKJV

Dad was angry from watching too many political shows on television. The almost sixteen-year-old thought his life was over because he hadn't had driver's education classes yet, so he couldn't get his license. The eleven-year-old was yelling because the almost sixteen-year-old punched him for . . . well, nobody quite knew why.

And Mom was angry that she just spent good money on a nice restaurant meal for these ungrateful monsters.

On arriving home, she grudgingly decided to start the birthday preparations and went to the kitchen to lay out ingredients for her older son's favorite cake. Within ten minutes, almost magically, the mood of the entire family changed.

The almost sixteen-year-old walked into the kitchen, saw the task at hand, and hugged his mom for making his cake, even after his poor behavior. The eleven-year-old was excited because Mom let him help mix the cake. Dad was happy because everyone else had quit fighting.

And Mom was amazed that the whole evening turned

on the baking of a cake—a small act of love.

We can never guess how important our slightest actions will be to those around us. As you go through the day, you have a choice in your interactions with everyone you meet. Choose the act of love.

The one who truly loves gives all and
sacrifices nothing.

RAINER MARIA RILKE

HIDDEN BLESSINGS

I t was a rough day at the office. Nancy was struggling with too many meetings, too many project deadlines, and not enough time to complete anything. Her performance review was due, and she feared the raise she needed was not going to happen.

What's more, her daughter had been out of school with respiratory flu for three days with no sign of improvement. Nancy and her husband, Tom, were rotating their office leave so someone would always be home with their child.

> In everything, give thanks; for this is the will of God in Christ Jesus for you.
>
> 1 THESSALONIANS 5:18 NKJV

Her phone rang. It was Tom calling, worried because their daughter's breathing was becoming labored. Nancy knew immediately that the child needed to see a doctor again, and she had to be there with her.

Racing home, she wanted to cry. *Why did everything have to happen at once?* she wondered. *When am I ever going to get a break?*

Suddenly, she was startled by a loud bang, as the car ahead of her blew a tire and slowly maneuvered to a nearby parking lot. Nancy took a deep breath to regain her composure and thought, *Okay, God, how bad off am I, really?*

As she picked up her daughter and sped to the emergency clinic, Nancy decided to concentrate on the things that were going right. She prayed to the Lord:

Thank You for good tires and cars that work.

Thank You for my job.

Thank You for doctors.

Thank You for insurance.

Thank You for helping my daughter to breathe.

Thank You for coming with me.

Thank You for showing me how much I have to be thankful for.

The finest test of character is seen in the amount and the power of gratitude we have.

MILO H. GATES

RULES? WHAT RULES?

"**W**hat do you mean, you don't have to go by rules?" Rick asked his daughter Heather, with a note of incredulity in his voice.

"Shelley said that we don't have to go by rules."

> "Blessed are the peacemakers: for they shall be called the children of God."
>
> MATTHEW 5:9 KJV

"Well, Shelley's wrong; you do have to go by rules."

"No, I don't. Shelley said so."

"Yes, you do!" he insisted.

The argument continued for a few minutes until Rick's wife, Jane, stepped into Heather's bedroom and quietly said, "Rick, do you realize that you are arguing with a three-year-old?" She then turned to their little girl and asked, "Heather, do you know what rules are?"

"No."

"When you're at school," she continued, "do you and Shelley ever need to line up so that your class can go to lunch or out to the playground?"

"Yes."

"Well, that's a rule."

"Oh, okay."

With a small smile, Jane hugged Heather and quietly

left the room. With a sheepish look on his face, Rick followed. "I guess I got carried away," he mumbled.

It's pretty easy to get carried away. In fact, if we are not careful, we can find ourselves embroiled in conflict with others without ever knowing why. Family feuds are often like that; the reason for the hatred has long since been forgotten, but the animosity continues from generation to generation. Continuing in such conflict without trying to understand one another is as senseless as Rick arguing with his three-year-old.

It took the loving voice of Heather's mother to calm the waters. We can be that voice, too, if we so desire. Remember, Jesus said, "Blessed are the peacemakers."

Gently to hear, kindly to judge.

WILLIAM SHAKESPEARE

GENTLE RIPPLES

> O God, you are my God; early will I seek you.
>
> PSALM 63:1
> NKJV

Early in the morning a lake is usually very still —no animals, no people, no noise, no boats, no cars. All is quiet.

This is the best time to skip rocks. By taking a small flat pebble and throwing it at the right angle, you can skip it across the water leaving circles of ripples every time it makes contact with the lake. The ripples form small and very defined circles at first; then they spread out and break apart until they vanish. If several people skip rocks at the same time, the ripples cross over one another and blend together to make mini-waves across the lake. The impact can be pretty amazing.

For most of us, mornings are filled with so many things that need our attention that we find it difficult to spend time alone with God. However, Christ set a marvelous example for us by rising early to listen to God. If we make no time for these quiet morning moments with God, we often find there is also no time during the day. Then we end up going to bed with regret or guilt. *Maybe tomorrow*, we think. But too many times, tomorrow never comes.

When we spend time alone with God at the beginning of each day, we become acquainted with Him and start becoming like Him. Throughout our days, the ripple effect of our time with God in the early morning will impact the lives of those with whom we have contact.

When these ripples blend with others who also spend time with God, we create mini-waves of love and joy. It all starts with a quiet time and a gentle ripple.

It is good to be alone in the garden at
dawn or dark so that all its shy presences
may haunt you and possess you in a
reverie of suspended thought.

JAMES DOUGLAS

THANK YOU, LORD

I t is easier to thank the Lord after we have seen His work, for we then have something to go back to and rejoice over. It is not as easy to be thankful for what we don't see or haven't experienced.

> I will give thanks to the Lord with all my heart.
>
> PSALM 9:1
> NASB

A mother purchased a new violin for her son. Together they had saved for months to be able to afford this fine instrument. He had promised to care for it, but it wasn't long before the boy had forgotten his promise and left his violin out on the porch overnight. The cold night air and the heavy morning dew caused the violin to bulge, and the sound quality was no longer the same.

The boy's mother took this opportunity to teach her son a lesson for life. She decided to show him what went into the making of the violin. She took him to the store where they had made the purchase. They then visited a manufacturing company where violins were produced and went to a lumber mill where the wood had been carefully chosen for such a fine instrument. They even visited a forest where trees were being grown specifically for quality instruments. The mother and son also made trips to learn how the bow and strings were manufactured. She wanted her son to understand why he should have been thankful for the beautiful musical instrument with which he had been blessed.

God wants our thanks, and He has provided us with

a never-ending supply of reminders of why we should be grateful to Him. Starting the day off in an attitude of gratefulness leaves little room for complaints and much room for grace to flourish.

A thankful heart is not only the greatest
virtue, but the parent of all other virtues.

CICERO

NEVER GIVE UP

Again, the young teacher read the note attached to the fresh green ivy: "Because of the seeds you planted, we will one day grow into beautiful plants like this one. We appreciate all you've done for us. Thank you for investing time in our lives."

A smile widened on the teacher's face as grateful tears trickled down her cheeks. Like the one leper who expressed gratitude to Jesus for healing him, the girls she had taught remembered to say thanks to their Sunday-school teacher. The ivy plant represented a gift of love. For months the teacher faithfully watered that growing plant. Each time she looked at it, she remembered those special teenagers and was encouraged to continue teaching.

But after a year, something happened. The leaves began to turn yellow and drop—all but one. She started to discard the ivy but decided instead to keep watering and fertilizing it. One day as she walked through the kitchen, the teacher noticed a new shoot on the plant. A few days later, another leaf appeared, and then another. Within a few months, the ivy was well on its way to becoming a healthy plant once again.

Let us not become weary in doing good,
for at the proper time we will reap a
harvest if we do not give up.

GALATIANS 6:9

Henry Drummond says, "Do not think that nothing is happening because you do not see yourself grow, or hear the whir of the machinery. All great things grow noiselessly."

Few joys exceed the blessings of faithfully investing time and love into the lives of others. Never, never give up on those plants!

The garden is never dead; growth is
always going on, and growth can be seen,
and seen with delight!

CANON HENRY ELLACOMBE

BELIEVE IN ME

Cynthia was amazed and grateful for what she was seeing. Ms. Nelson, a fifth grade teacher at the private school where Cynthia worked, was quietly greeting the children and their parents at the door of her classroom. Ms. Nelson spoke with pride to each parent of the work of his or her child. She took time to mention the child by name and to point out something on that child's work that was particularly noteworthy. As a result, both the parent and the child glowed with satisfaction.

> The Lord make you to increase and abound in love one toward another, and toward all men.
>
> 1 THESSALONIANS 3:12 KJV

This was not a special event — it was the morning of a normal school day, and Ms. Nelson made it a habit to be at the door every morning.

As Cynthia stepped into her own office, she was struck by the impact of Ms. Nelson's genuine comments and actions. She couldn't help but think of a gardener fussing over the flowers and plants of the garden — eager to provide the right nourishment and attention so that each plant grows strong and healthy.

Later that afternoon, Cynthia asked her fifth-grade son, John, how he liked being in Ms. Nelson's class. John responded, "I like it a lot. She's a really neat teacher because you always know that she believes in you. Even when you don't get everything right, she still believes in you."

What a gift—the ability to believe in others and communicate it to them daily, just as our Lord loves and believes in us without fail! We can all learn to pass this gift on to those we care about.

Encouragement is oxygen to the soul.

GEORGE M. ADAMS

CHILDLIKE THINKING

I t had been years since the four siblings had been together, and the air was filled with laughter as they entertained their families with stories from their childhood. The three older brothers told story after story of the trials and tribulations of having three boys in one bedroom. They also told of the many practical jokes they played on one another and of the numerous fights they had had as kids. But no one could top Sherry's story of being the "baby sister."

> Brethren, be not children in understanding.
>
> 1 CORINTHIANS 14:20 KJV

"You know, guys," she said during a momentary lull in the conversation, "I used to think that with future generations all people were born girls and would eventually turn into boys. In fact, I used to wonder when I would become a boy just like you guys." She then laughed and firmly stated, "Thank goodness that didn't happen."

When she was just a child, Sherry's concept made perfect sense. She had three older brothers and no sisters, so naturally she assumed she would one day become a boy too. Of course, as she grew old enough to understand things better, this idea slipped away to become just a fond memory.

While physical growth and maturation occur independent of our control, how many times do we remain "children in our understanding" because we simply choose not to exercise our thinking abilities or because the issues we must face are just too uncomfortable? Yet we can seek God's wisdom and direction so that we might grow in our understanding of His desires for us.

Are you willing to accept that challenge today?

If there were no difficulties there would
be no triumphs.

B. C. FORBES

GROW UP!

"Grow up!" is a taunt often used by teenagers to their peers who, for whatever reason, aren't acting as mature as they should at the moment. The command is given with the attitude that the immature person can simply make a choice to immediately grow up.

> He will be like a tree firmly planted by streams of water, which yields its fruit in its season.
>
> PSALM 1:3 NASB

Commanding a friend to "grow up" doesn't do any more good than telling a tree to "grow up." There is a process that must take place, and that process takes time. Every living thing requires certain elements in order to grow—good soil, the appropriate amounts of sunshine and water, and plenty of time.

People, like trees, need a good start in order to be rooted securely. Young saplings can't mature into beautiful and tall shade trees without the right mixture of sun, water, rich soil, and space. As long as a tree is living, it never stops growing and never outgrows its need for nourishment. Most importantly, this process takes time—and lots of it.

In God's perfect timing, we will indeed "grow up." Like babies taking their first steps, so we must be willing to let nature takes its course. The growth process is a long one, and it never really is complete. Flourishing trees don't strain to grow. They merely follow the natural process God planted in them. And healthy trees don't decide to just ignore the nourishment of sun, rain, and soil. Instead, they continually draw life from these things.

No matter what our "season" of life, we are wise to remember that growing up is a continuous process—and it all happens in God's time.

———————————————

Like the roots of a plant, faith must seek greater depth or be subject to the law of death.

JOHN POWELL

JUST LIKE DADDY

T he snow-covered peaks, fragrant evergreens, and a rustic lodge combined to create a picture-perfect postcard scene. Inside the adjacent condo, a grandmother kept her five-month-old granddaughter while the baby's parents took their turn skiing. After Emily had her nap, bottle, and playtime, the grandmother then zipped her into a feather-soft blue bunting and carried her toward the lobby to await the family's return.

> God create man in his own image. In the image of God he created him: male and female he created them.
>
> GENESIS 1:27
> NASB

Other guests and hotel workers began smiling when they saw the baby. They approached her, talked baby talk, and reached out to touch her chubby cheeks. Emily's flawless skin and innocent blue eyes captured everyone's attention. Big strong athletic skiers paused to coo with her. Seasoned seniors who had seen decades of history delighted in her innocence. Weary travelers paused from their hectic schedules to smile and "talk" with her.

The shuttle bus soon pulled into the driveway. As Emily's parents entered the lobby, she recognized them and squealed with delight. A lady sitting nearby commented, "Why, little girl, you look just like your daddy!" Everyone chuckled because it was true. Although only a little face peered from the bunting, anyone—even a stranger — could see the strong resemblance.

When people see us, does our joy overflow to them? Do we delight the hearts of people who cross our paths? Does the image of our Heavenly Daddy reflect in the light of our eyes? Will people recognize Him? Whom do we look like?

Let each man think himself an act of God, his mind a thought of God, his life a breath of God.

PHILIP JAMES BAILEY

CHILD'S PLAY

P rofessional golfer Tiger Woods was considered one of the top players of the 1990s, with the potential to rank among the greatest of all time. Watching him line up a forty-foot downhill breaking putt, some may recall seeing him on the Tonight Show when he was about three years of age.

Tiger was already showing a talent for the game, so a small putting surface was set up for him. A ball was placed in front of him, about eight feet from the cup. He lined up the shot, putted, and missed.

Another ball was placed in the same position. He again prepared to putt — then picked the ball up, placed it six inches from the cup, and promptly sank the shot. Johnny Carson and the audience laughed and cheered to see a small child do what many adults would like to do. Of course, if he did that today, he would be ejected from the tournament.

A resident of a small town was once asked by a tourist: "Have any famous people been born here?"

He replied, "No, only babies."

... until we all reach unity in the faith and in the knowledge of the Son of God and become mature, attaining to the whole measure of the fullness of Christ.

EPHESIANS 4:13

We all start out as "only babies," but our Creator has placed within us the greatest power in the universe: the ability to grow, day by day, as we respond to increasing challenges.

How will you meet your challenges today? You can either grow more selfish, more reclusive, more pessimistic, and more filled with hate. Or, with the help of God, you can grow to be more understanding, optimistic, giving, and loving. You have been given this day to grow. Will you do it your way or His?

There are no great men in this world,
only great challenges which ordinary men
rise to meet.

WILLIAM FREDERICK HALSEY JR.

TEXAS LIMESTONE

"Other fell on good ground, and did yield fruit."

MARK 4:8 KJV

Anita was determined to have a garden. She spent the entire hot, humid afternoon hacking away at the small plot of ground in the back of their central Texas home. In the vernacular of farmers, it was "poor" soil—incapable of sustaining even the hardiest of vegetables. After about three inches, the soil gave way to limestone. But that was not going to stop her! She just grew more stubborn as she shoveled her way through the rocks.

Every time it seemed that she had found the last rock, sparks would fly from the blade as she again struck limestone. She grew weary and was tempted to give up her garden. The ground was just too hard and the soil too scarce. It seemed that nothing would grow in this place. Yet she longed for a garden filled with ripe red tomatoes, green cucumbers, tall okra, and big ears of corn.

Slowly, the soil began to turn more easily. Occasionally, she would use the garden hose to dampen the dry earth as she removed the rocks. Finally the rocks were removed. She then mixed in bags of new, rich topsoil and shaped the soil into nice smooth, parallel rows. At last, the garden was ready for her to plant the vegetable seeds.

Like her garden, Anita had to work hard to keep her heart right and free from the burdensome rocks of unforgiveness. She longed for healthy, merciful soil where

seeds of God's love would yield a bumper crop of compassion and kindness. She knew that her daily choices
in thought, word, and deed would determine whether
her heart-garden was full of bitter rocks or joyful vegetation.

Forgiveness is not an occasional act; it is a
permanent attitude.

MARTIN LUTHER KING JR.

THE CONTEST

I t was a typical day in first grade, and while their teacher was tending to other students, Sammy and Molly were engrossed in a discussion of the utmost importance: Who was taller?

> The child grew and became strong, filled with wisdom; and the favor of God was upon him.
>
> LUKE 2:40 RSV

Molly was one of the smaller children in the class, but that never interfered with her keen sense of competition. When Sammy declared his superior height, she responded by sitting up tall and straight. When Sammy sat up taller and straighter, Molly stood up beside her desk. When Sammy stood up across the aisle and immediately overshadowed her, Molly—after stealing a glance across the room to ensure her teacher's back was still turned—stepped up on her chair.

When the teacher finally turned to check on the commotion, the two children were standing atop their desks on their tiptoes, stretching for all they were worth!

Children are typically excited about growing bigger, and the wise adult continues to seek internal growth. Those who lose this zest die long before their funerals.

How long has it been since you felt the thrill of growing—of improving some aspect of your life? You may have felt it as you graduated from high school, received your first promotion on the job, learned a new craft, or ran in your first 5K race. The desire for growth is a powerful incentive in our lives.

If improving in size, career, or talent is exciting, other aspects of our lives can bring even more lasting satisfaction. Growing in our relationship with God is one of them. In fact, taking our desires for growth to the Lord can result in a double blessing — gaining His strength and vision for improving our lives, while deepening our joy in knowing Him.

A state of mind that sees God in
everything is evidence of growth in grace
and a grateful heart.

CHARLES G. FINNEY

A GARDEN OF HOPE

As Shannon sat by her mother's bedside day by day, she observed the leaves changing to autumn splendor outside the bedroom window. And each day, she watched her mother's cancer-riddled body weaken.

One by one, the green leaves outside faded to yellow, then bright orange, covering the ground like a pool of liquid sunshine. One morning a north gust of wind blew through the back garden where the oak tree stood. Its limbs, now naked and lonely, swayed in the winter breeze.

As Shannon looked out the window one morning, she noticed a lone leaf hanging on tenaciously. The same day, her mother's pulse grew weaker, and she slipped into a coma. All that week, Shannon struggled. She longed to hear her mother's words once again—to feel the spring-time of her voice and to whisper "I love you" again to her.

> See, I am doing a new thing! Now it springs up; do you not perceive it?
>
> ISAIAH 43:19

Outside the bedroom window, the lone leaf held on. Shannon wondered how it could keep from fluttering to the ground. An inner voice seemed to murmur the answer: *It needs to let go, and so do you.*

The next morning Shannon walked quietly into her mother's room, dreading to see her lifeless form. But her mom suddenly woke up, squeezed her daughter's hand,

and said, "I love you, Shannon."

"Oh, Mom. I love you too."

And then, like a leaf that had clung too long, her mother released Shannon's hand—and she was gone.

As Shannon closed the drapes that afternoon, she realized the leaf had disappeared from the old oak tree. But in its place, a new bud was already forming. Shannon knew joy would blossom again. Like the promise of springtime, God would grow a new garden of hope in the fertile soil of Shannon's heart.

Love comforteth like sunshine after rain.

WILLIAM SHAKESPEARE

SECRET GARDENS

*T*he *Secret Garden*, by Frances Hodgson Burnett, beautifully illustrates the power of kindness and faith. Collin, the adolescent son of a rich, but grieving father who cannot rebound from his wife's death, lives his days as a demanding, selfish invalid. At first, Collin rejects the friendly gestures of Mary, his long-lost cousin. When young Mary discovers the key to a secret garden on the grounds of her uncle's estate, she also opens a hidden door to her own heart's joys. She immediately sets out to restore the garden's long-lost magic and beauty.

> This land that was laid waste has become like the garden of eden.
>
> EZEKIEL 36:35

Little by little, Mary persuades Collin to take another step toward healing and unselfishness. Her stubborn persistence finally prevails on Collin to spend time outside in the restored garden, which had been lovingly planted by his late mother. Strength seeps back into the young boy's life and changes his saddened, bitter heart. The garden seems to work like magic on the young boy as he is restored, not only in body and spirit, but also in relationship with his distant father.

Untended souls can hide for years, as bitter thorns grow, choking out the life and obscuring the beauty that lies within. But as we gently clear away the rubble of the past and cut through the neglected gardens of people's hearts, we make a remarkable discovery—lives, sweet and beautiful, waiting to be filled with the divine fragrance of Heaven. There are potential "gardens" all around us — in our neighborhoods, in our schools, in our homes, and at work. We have been given the key, and it is no secret what virtual gardens of Eden we can help uncover as we share God's love freely with others.

To love abundantly is to live forever.

HENRY DRUMMOND

BLACK MOUNTAIN

"I will just run away to Black Mountain!" screamed five-year-old Richard.

"Okay, if that's what you want, go ahead," responded his mother, opening the door and ushering him out to the front porch.

The silence descended on him like a cloak. The sun was long gone, and full night had settled upon the landscape. By the starlight he could just make out the dark form of Black Mountain to the north. Somewhere in the darkness, he heard the scurrying of a small animal and then the flap of wings in the night sky. Suddenly, his small heart was pounding in his chest, and his breath was coming quicker. Going to Black Mountain seemed like a really bad idea. He thought, *Why did I say that?*

> Many are the plans in a man's heart, but it is the Lord's purpose that prevails.
>
> PROVERBS 19:21

He sat on the porch with his knees drawn up to his chest and arms clasped around them. A tear trickled down his cheek as he tried to fight off his fears.

From the kitchen, he heard his father ask, "Richard, would you like to come to supper with the rest of us now?"

Sometimes when we get angry with ourselves, others, circumstances, or even God, we want to run away. We stomp out our anger, and we make threats. We go out on the porch and pout. Yet, the Father waits patiently and even gently calls to us to rejoin the family. Love chases away fears, and restoration heals hurts.

Anger is quieted by a gentle word just as
fire is quenched by water.

JEAN PIERRE CAMUS

TIME FOR BED

Teach me thy
way, O Lord.

PSALM 27:11 KJV

When children are around two years old, many of them decide that staying up past their regular bedtime is something worth creating havoc over. These little replicas of ourselves come up with every conceivable excuse to stay awake, no matter how tired they may actually be. From the tenth drink of water, to the fifth bathroom trip, to the whining about what's behind the door (or under the bed), to the "I love you sooooooo much, Mommy and Daddy," to the fits of anger — these little ones try to get something that they can't yet handle responsibly.

Parents read books, complain to their child's pediatrician, consult with their minister, whine to their own friends, and disagree with their spouse about the right way to handle this annoying situation. In some cases the child may gain the upper hand and stay up too late, smiling gleefully while sitting between Mom and Daddy on the sofa, watching TV, and eating popcorn.

At this stage in their lives, two-year-olds are test-driving their ability to assert their own opinions and desires, the first step to autonomy. It is the parents' responsibility to guide those desires with a balance of freedom and discipline. Physiologically, two-year-olds need more sleep than ten-year-olds or thirty-year-olds. Their growing bodies need time to rest in order to properly support each day's whirlwind of activity. The privilege of staying up later truly is only something that can be earned with time.

Like toddlers, sometimes we want something that we are not yet prepared to handle. We might not like it much, but sometimes we just have to trust God to know what is best for us. If we ask God for wisdom in balancing our lives, He is sure to help us.

Don't try to hold God's hand; let him
hold yours. Let him do the holding, and
you the trusting.

HAMMER WILLIAM WEBB-PEPLOE

LET ME DO IT
BY MYSELF!

Five-year-old Lili would often fluctuate from "Let me do it by myself" to "Mommy, help me," in a matter of moments. Tying her shoes, buttoning her sweater, pouring her milk, riding her bicycle, and brushing her hair seemed to be her rites of passage.

> Bring up a child in the way he should go. Even when he is old he will not depart from it.
>
> PROVERBS 22:6 NASB

Her mother seldom knew whether it was all right to lend unsolicited assistance or to let the youngster work independently. When safety was an issue, the answer was obvious. "No, honey. Mommy has to help you with baking cookies (or crossing the street or reaching a top shelf), because I don't want you to get hurt. When you're bigger, you can do this by yourself." Because Lili was allowed lots of opportunities to do the safe things on her own, it helped to take the sting out of the temporary no she got on the unsafe ones.

We say no to our children because we love them. And when the time is right, we can also say yes because we love them. It takes wisdom and knowledge to train a child. No might be the best answer to a request today that might change to a yes tomorrow after some instruction and practice.

Growing up is not easy. We have life lessons from

cradle to grave. Like our children, we need guidance in knowing how to do certain things. While we always need God's help, some decisions or circumstances require double doses of His guidance.

From that first "no-no" spoken to a toddler who is about to touch a hot stove to that moment when we reluctantly slip the car keys into our teen's hand, are tucked away years of training. If we have taught and loved our children well, we can confidently say, "Yes, you and God can do it by yourselves."

Confidence is a plant of slow growth.

ENGLISH PROVERB

WHAT AM I KNOWN FOR?

"What does it matter other people think of me? I don't care about them anyway!" Rebecca blurted out to her mom. "Why are you so concerned that I finish the service project in Girl Scouts, anyway? I'm gonna quit Scouts next year, and besides I already have plenty of badges."

"Scouting and badges are not the issues," her mother replied. "I'm concerned with you and what you are known for. You are very caring and compassionate, warm and loving. You care deeply for the welfare of others. You made a commitment to the people at the assisted living facility, and many of them look forward to you visiting them. It's just hard for me to see you not keeping a promise."

"But, I'm tired of going up there every Saturday," Rebecca said.

Her mother suggested that they find a way to reduce some of her time commitment without abandoning the promise. Before long, Rebecca felt that she could complete the commitment without giving up all of her free time.

> "Every tree is known by his own fruit. For of thorns men do not gather figs, nor of a bramble bush gather they grapes."
>
> LUKE 6:44 KJV

Later she commented to a friend that she hoped she would always live up to her mom's belief in her to be caring, compassionate, and trustworthy.

We are known more by what we do than by what we say. Sometimes commitments are overwhelming, particularly during the holidays or when pressures at work, home, church, or community seem to stretch us to the limit. Setting priorities and living by them—and most importantly, asking God for wisdom—will help us keep our promises without losing our heart.

Nothing is particularly hard if you divide
it into small jobs.

HENRY FORD

WALKING IN THE GARDEN

Sleeping in was not a common occurrence for Patti growing up on a farm, not even during summer vacation from school. But Patti's mother allowed her children to sleep in once in a great while. On those rare occasions, Patti awakened gently to the smells and sounds of her mother lovingly preparing a delicious family breakfast. The aroma of sizzling bacon frying wafted through the house. Pots and pans clattered. Fresh biscuits baking in the oven provided gentle nudges to help the children shake off their slumber.

> They heard the sound of the Lord God walking in the garden.
>
> GENESIS 3:8
> NASB

One summer morning, the house was still. Patti's brothers and sisters were sound asleep, and the kitchen was void of the usual sights, sounds, and smells of meal preparation. Patti noticed that the back door was open, and she slowly eased her way out to the back porch. There she caught a glimpse of her mother weeding the garden, humming all the while. The peaceful scene wrapped itself around Patti like a cozy blanket as she watched her mother walking in the garden.

Adam and Eve lived in the only perfect garden. They could commune with nature freely, and they walked and talked with the Lord face-to-face. They heard His sounds as He walked in the garden toward them. In her spirit, Patti's mother must have known the sweetness of God's

148

presence as she walked in her garden early in the morning. Before the demands of her day busied her hands and her mind, she wisely chose the morning quiet for a peaceful walk with God in the garden.

Sweet is the garden, white with bloom,
heavy with honey, drenched with scent.

KATHARINE TYNAN HINKSON

A SEASON OF LOVE

I n his book *Fatherhood*, Bill Cosby shares his humorous views on parenting:

We . . . did not have (children) because we thought it would be fun to see one of them sit in a chair and stick out his leg so that another one of them running by was launched like Explorer I.

After which I said to the child who was the launching pad, "Why did you do that?"

"Do what?" he replied.

"Stick out your leg."

"Dad, I didn't know my leg was going out. My leg, it does that a lot."

Cosby says, "If you cannot function in a world where things like this are said, then you better forget about raising children and go to daffodils."[26]

In fact, raising children is a lot like growing daffodils. Children, like those colorful bulbs, will bloom where they are planted. But they only bloom for a season.

Just ask Bill Cosby. In spite of his tongue-in-cheek tales about parenting, he loved his son Ennis dearly but was granted only a season in which to enjoy him. An apparent robber killed Ennis in the prime of his youth.

Our children are God's gifts to us. Though they move out of our homes, they will never grow out of the garden of our hearts. Like spring daffodils, the memories of their childhood reappear continually.

Enjoy them while you can.

Love every day. Each one is so short and
they are so few.

NORMAN VINCENT PEALE

HOLY LAUGHTER

T he air was filled with peals of laughter along with giggles of delight and chortles of joy. Just hearing it made Ron's day better. His mother had run a licensed day-care facility in their home for as long as he could remember, and dozens of children from single-parent households benefited from her unconditional love. In fact, it was easy to think of their home as an oasis of love in a world lacking in it.

> He will yet fill your mouth with laughter and your lips with shouts of joy.
>
> JOB 8:21

Ron remembered the December morning when four- year-old Louis came in from the cold and quite seriously said, "It's winter out there, Reen (short for Irene)!" as he struggled to pull his arms free from his heavy coat.

Or there was the time when Jeffrey came by to visit and hand deliver an invitation to his high school graduation. "Grandma Reen" had cared for him throughout his elementary school years. Ron remembered Jeffrey coming from school each day of third grade. He and his best friend would exit the school with their arms draped around one another's shoulders, and they would walk that way all the way to the car.

Many, many other memories existed. But the best, without a doubt, was that of the joyous laughter of the children as they played together. There was something so natural and carefree about the sound that anyone who heard it would know that this place was a world of safety and love — thanks to "Grandma Reen."

Have you had the chance to listen to the laughter of small children lately? Take time to listen, and your soul will be refreshed.

Laughter is the most beautiful and
beneficial therapy God ever granted
humanity.

CHARLES R. SWINDOLL

NIGHTS WITH MOM

Saturday evenings had a special, even magical quality to them for young Kevin. In fact, he could hardly wait for them to come. The routine was nearly always the same, and it made his world safe and predictable.

First, the family would share a casual supper together. This meal would nearly always be homemade hamburgers, French fries, and cold pork-and-beans. The table would include condiments for the hamburgers, napkins for the milk mustaches, and conversation for the heart. It was a time of love and closeness. To this day, homemade hamburgers remind Kevin of his childhood.

After supper, he would polish everyone's Sunday dress shoes at one end of the kitchen table, while at the other end, his mother prepared her Sunday school lesson for the next day.

She taught a class for young children, so she used flannel-graph characters to tell the Bible stories. As she cut out the characters and rehearsed the lessons, Kevin would listen in; the stories seemed to come alive. He saw David slay Goliath, Joseph sold into slavery by his broth-

I am reminded of your sincere faith, which first lived in your grandmother Lois and in your mother Eunice and, I am persuaded, now lives in you also.

2 TIMOTHY 1:5

ers, Moses leading the Israelites across the Red Sea, and many more great events so vital to the Christian heritage and faith.

It is simply amazing how much of Kevin's own faith story was learned right there as he polished shoes and listened to his mother. To this day, the smell of shoe polish brings back warm memories and bolsters his faith.

Pray for the seeds of divine truth to be planted in the fertile minds and hearts of your children today. Pray that they will stand firm in the faith as they grow old.

Faith is not belief without proof, but
trust without reservations.

ELTON TRUEBLOOD

GROWING IN WISDOM

After their wedding, the young couple prepared for their move from Ireland to America. It meant leaving their families behind and starting from scratch in a new country, but they were committed for the long haul. Even though many from their village came and settled close to them, it didn't take long for the newlyweds to realize that the man's trade would not allow him to provide for his family. What could have been the justification for a speedy retreat back to Dublin was, instead, the fuel that fired the determination to learn a new skill and prove he could provide for his family against all odds.

> A wise man will hear and increase in learning, and a man of understanding will acquire wise counsel.
>
> PROVERBS 1:5 NASB

He and his wife agreed that Christ would be their Strength and Guide for the uphill battle that lay ahead. They decided that until a new skill was mastered, everything else had to take a back seat except their love and devotion to God and to each other.

The man bought a used typewriter, an adding machine, and several textbooks. After his regular job ended every day, he would sit until the wee hours of the next morning, studying, pecking away at both machines until he had taught himself how to type proficiently and how to do the work of a master accountant.

His work became so well known that for the rest of his life he was in constant demand. It was said that his work was the finest in the land. He and his family lived very comfortable lives, and he left a legacy to his children and others of a man who was willing to listen, learn, and grow in wisdom.

True wisdom consists not only in seeing
what is before our eyes, but in foreseeing
what is to come.

TERENCE

FIELD OF DREAMS

Hope deferred makes the heart sick, but a longing fulfilled is a tree of life.

PROVERBS
13:12

There was nothing special about Randy. Each year his teachers repeated the same words: "You don't want Randy in your class. Lie's a loser."

But that was before he entered Miss Jewel's sixth grade art class. Until then, only bright red Ds and Fs adorned Randy's school papers. Test scores plummeted him to the bottom 10 percent of his class.

Miss Jewel saw the sparkle in Randy's eyes when he watched her demonstrations. His huge, rough fingers took to a paintbrush like an athlete to sports. Charcoals, clay, watercolor, oils—whatever the project, he excelled beyond any student Miss Jewel had ever seen.

She challenged him to take private lessons and suggested the names of several artists she knew. Randy made excuses for not pursuing the lessons, but she suspected it was because of his family's poverty.

The teacher decided to make Randy her special project. Year after year she saved her money. On his graduation from high school, she sent him an anonymous check to cover his college tuition—and the name of an artist who agreed to teach him in the summers between his college studies.

One day about ten years later, she received a package in the mail—a beautiful oil painting of herself and a note with these words: "I will never forget you. I have dedicated my life to helping others grow their dreams like you did for me. Thank you, Randy."

God may give each of us "Randys" to nurture—perhaps children, friends, students, or coworkers. Our words, our time, even our belief in their abilities could help produce a crop of doctors, musicians, presidents, or simply loving moms and dads who will rise in their own "field of dreams."

Quality is never an accident; it is always
the result of intelligent effort.

JOHN RUSKIN

GARDEN VARIETY PLAYERS

For years, Daron dreamed of playing basketball. He practiced daily after school. His dad bought a backboard and goal, and together they shot hoops in the driveway. In his freshman year of high school, Daron failed to make the basketball team. Discouraged but refusing to quit, he kept practicing and attended all the games. He hung around after school and watched the guys practice. In his sophomore year, he tried out again. This time he made the team but sat on the bench most of the year. But he kept on practicing.

> Now you are the body of Christ, and each one of you is a part of it.
>
> 1 CORINTHIANS 12:27

As a junior, Daron finally got his break and became a regular on the starting lineup. Although he could hit 75 percent of his shots, the coach rarely changed the rules: "Get the ball to Jim—as much as you can." Jim was the star of most games. He won the Most Valuable Player every year for three years and received a complete scholarship to a nearby college.

Daron expected no scholarship. After all, he was just a garden variety player. One day a coach from a prestigious university out of state called him, offering him a full scholarship.

"Why would you want me?" Daron asked.

"We've watched videos of you and your team in action, and we're impressed with your team skills. Lots of guys can be a star. But it takes a team — and a team player — to win successive games."

We may feel like "garden variety" Christians, being used in only small ways. We wonder how we could be making a difference. But God is not in the business of recruiting "star" players. What He wants is a faithful heart, willing to serve Him as Heaven's team player.

———————————————

Faithfulness in little things is a big thing.

SAINT JOHN CHRYSOSTOM

THE ART OF CULTIVATION

"What's this, Grandpa?" asked ten-year-old Samantha.

She was exploring the contents of the garage and had come across a very strange device. It had a long handle like a rake or shovel, but on the end was a round rubber wheel with a funny attachment consisting of two interlocking circles of steel teeth. When she tried to roll it on the concrete floor, the steel teeth prevented the rubber wheel from touching the floor, and it made an awful racket.

> The secrets of his heart will be laid bare.
>
> 1 CORINTHIANS 14:25

Turning from his workbench, Grandpa Bill smiled. "Sweetheart, that's a cultivator, and it's used in our garden. Those teeth break up the surface of the soil and uproot weeds. Breaking up the soil allows water and nutrients to get to the roots of our vegetables, and getting rid of the weeds allows them to grow freely."

"Wow, Grandpa, that's neat. Our Sunday school teacher was telling us the story of how a man's enemy put bad seeds in his wheat, and then weeds grew up. If they would have had a cultivator like this, they could have removed the weeds without waiting until the harvest."

"Yes, you're right," Bill replied. "The hard soil and weeds in my life need cultivating too. When something is not good for me, I have to clean those 'spiritual weeds' out of my life."

"I never thought of it that way before, Grandpa. When I do wrong and then I feel bad, is God just getting my attention now so I can do it better next time?"

"Yes," Grandpa Bill replied. "He uproots the bad weeds in our hearts and breaks up the soil so He can plant good things."

God wills us free, man wills us slaves, I
will as God wills, God's will be done.

DANIEL BLISS

FREEDOM TO DANCE

It is for freedom that Christ has set us free. Stand firm, then, and do not let yourselves be burdened again by a yoke of slavery.

GALATIANS 5:1

As a child, Ellen loved her Uncle Merrill's garden. The plants that captured her attention most were the hundreds of white gladioli planted in long, straight rows just like Uncle Merrill's sweet corn. It frustrated Ellen, however, when a breeze forced the tall, slender flowers to sway out of position. She preferred to see them standing tall and erect instead of dancing in the breeze.

As Ellen grew into adulthood, she tried to make her life perfect like Uncle Merrill's rows of sweet corn instead of his dancing gladioli. She tried with all her might to march a narrow, straight line, but she constantly swayed out of the rigid position.

One day in utter frustration, she cried out to God, "I can't do it! These rules are too heavy a burden." After a good cry, she decided to go see Uncle Merrill.

Ellen sat in her car a long time watching Uncle Merrill's white gladioli weave back and forth in the breeze. Slowly she began to see that although the flowers freely danced in the sunshine, they remained firmly rooted in the soil. Those stalks of glorious white blossoms proclaimed to her a joyous message. If her heart is firmly rooted in Christ, she is free to rejoice in her faith. When

Ellen attempted to abide by a lengthy list of harsh rules, she realized she was choosing slavery when God had already set her free.

Finally, she understood that God's yoke of love is gentle, and His burden is light. Like the gladioli, she could dance freely in a summer breeze because of His incredible mercy.

Love is never satisfied with doing or giving anything but the best.

REVEREND J. M. GIBBON

PLANTING FOR
A LIFETIME

Eight-year-old Ray looked with open adoration and love at his pastor. He was an unremarkable man in many ways—small and thin with a wisp of hair on top of his head. To Ray though, Pastor Majors was right next to God in holiness. He was gentle, with a kind, loving heart, and with his eyes closed, he now played hymns on his harmonica.

> "You are the light of the world."
>
> MATTHEW 5:14

Pastor Majors could recite any verse in the entire Bible. God had blessed him with a "photographic memory" of the Holy Scripture. He never read aloud from the Bible; he only recited it. One Sunday evening he shared a story from his own youth that planted seeds of faith and courage in Ray's heart—seeds that would take root and stay with him for a lifetime.

"I was in high school when I broke my neck," the pastor said. "I was on the top of a school bus packing the band instruments to leave on a trip when I fell off and landed on my head. It was my faith in God that allowed me to recover and play music again."

The story impacted Ray's life deeply. His pastor's story of faith as a teenager helped him grow faith in his own heart over the course of his lifetime.

We never know when what we say will have a life-lasting impact. Henry George said, "Let no man imagine that he has no influence."[27] We cannot stop our influence, but we can choose which types of seeds we will plant.

Faith is power to believe and power to
see.

PRENTICE MULFORD

THE BIRTHDAY

Eleven-year-old Will hurried ahead of the rest of the party as they arrived at the restaurant for dinner to celebrate his mother's birthday. When everyone else came through the door, he had already spoken to the hostess, informing her that they would need a table for a party of seven in the nonsmoking section. The table was waiting, and the group quickly sat down. Throughout the dinner, Will, seated between his two grandfathers, was engaging and polite. He and his grandfathers seemed to share a secret as they whispered to each other off and on during dinner. He smiled often at his mother and winked knowingly.

> The righteous shall flourish.
>
> PSALM 92:12 KJV

Finally, as dinner came to a conclusion, the waiter arrived at the table with a beautifully presented and delicious serving of cheesecake topped with fresh berries. The dessert was for Will's mother for her birthday. Coffee cups were refilled and fresh forks provided as she shared the wonderful dessert with her family. Will, grinning, giggling, and outright laughing, clapped his hands and said, "Now you know why I was winking, don't ya, Mom!"

Later Will's parents commented on what a delightful young man he was becoming. It hardly seemed possible that this was the same little boy who, just a few short years earlier, had been so shy and withdrawn that you could barely get him to say hello to a waiter. Now, he was making arrangements for the entire dinner party.

Spiritual growth is just like that too. When we surround ourselves with other believers, study God's Word, attend worship, and pray faithfully, we cannot help but grow in the Lord. And as we grow in Christ, we naturally become a blessing to others and serve as a spirit of encouragement.

We can never be lilies in the garden
unless we have spent time as bulbs in the
dark, totally ignored.

OSWALD CHAMBERS

FAULTY BUT FAMILIAR

In all the travels of the Israelites, whenever the cloud lifted from above the tabernacle, they would set out . . .

EXODUS 40:36

"The Israelites had this cloud, Mom," Ellie's six-year-old exclaimed as the children tumbled into the car after Sunday school. "It was bigger than a thunderhead."

"Yeah, and at night it had fire in it brighter than a street light, so no one had to be afraid of the dark," echoed Ellie's timid four-year-old as she recalled the details of the Bible story they had heard.

"Every time the cloud moved, the people had to move," the six-year-old continued. "That would be great. You wouldn't be stuck in the same campground for forty years!"

Their spirited chattering continued on the short drive home as they shared that the Israelites never knew how long they would be in one campsite. Whenever God's cloud began to move, the Israelites were required to pack up and move too.

Moving would mean tearing your household apart. Every housewife in Israel would have to quickly dry the dishes, tear down her kitchen, repack the pots and pans, load everything onto the donkey cart, and follow after God's cloud. Then, when the cloud stopped, everything would have to be unloaded, unpacked, and re-set.

As Ellie walked into her kitchen that day, she took a close look at the linoleum that was gouged in places and the cupboards that were in need of another coat of paint. The contents of the overfilled trash can formed a precarious pyramid. The faucet still dripped annoyingly, and the dishes from breakfast sat piled on the counter. Yet with all its faults and peculiarities, it was home.

As her family bustled off to other parts of the house, Ellie sat down quietly at the kitchen table. "Thank You, God, for my kitchen," she said out loud. "I don't care if it does have drips and gouges and flaws. At least it's a kitchen that stays in one place!"

Home, the spot of earth supremely blest,
a dearer sweeter spot than all the rest.

ROBERT MONTGOMERY

PENNY FROM HEAVEN

K evin brushed the sandy-colored hair from his eyes and said, "Mom, I have a chance to be president of the fourth grade!" He reached for a cinnamon roll and poured some milk into a glass.

> Some trust in chariots and some in horses, but we trust in the name of the Lord our God.
>
> PSALM 20:7

"You know, Son, that it'll be a tough race."

The boy took a swallow of milk and wiped his face with his sleeve. "I know, Mom. But I just know I can do it."

His mother reached into the pocket of her jeans and pulled out a penny. "I tell you what, why don't you take my penny from Heaven to keep your spirits up?"

The boy grinned and put the penny in his pocket. He gathered his books and stuck them haphazardly into his book bag, then slung the bag over his shoulder.

Adrienne busied herself with everyday chores, wondering if her little boy would come home disappointed by failure or elated by victory. When 3:15 finally arrived, she was ready with his favorite chocolate chip cookies.

Kevin banged in the back door, his face beaming. He tugged on his baseball cap and cocked his head to one side. "I did it, Mom!" he said. "I'm the new president of the fourth-grade class!" He caught his breath and settled down in front of his plate of cookies. With his mouth full, he said, "I can't believe it, Mom! I just can't believe it!"

"I can," said his mother.

The boy looked puzzled. "What do you mean?"

"Take out that penny I gave you, and read what it says above Abraham Lincoln's head."

A radiant smile spread over her son's face as he read out loud, "In God We Trust!"

What are you putting your trust in? If it's material things, remember, they are only temporary. Instead, put your trust in God and His eternal life. He will never fail you.[28]

Trust God for great things; with your five loaves and two fishes. He will show you a way to feed thousands.

HORACE BUSHNELL

A PACKAGE OR A GUT?

A gaily-wrapped package rested on the kitchen counter. Having spent several days looking for just the right birthday present, Leslie knew her daughter would be pleased with the contents of the box. As she and her friends streamed through the back door after school, Leslie heard their exclamations — "Open it, Steph! It must be for you!"

> The gift of God is eternal life in Christ Jesus our Lord.
>
> ROMANS 6:23

She joined the excited girls and smiled at the surprised look on her daughter's face. "It's so pretty; I almost hate to open it," her daughter said. "Maybe I should wait until later."

"No!" her friends cried, urging her to open the package immediately to see what was inside.

Armed with their encouragement, Stephanie grinned and tore off the wrappings. Prying open the small box, she gasped and quickly gave her mother a kiss. "It's just what I wanted!" she cried as she pulled the stuffed animal out of the tissue paper and showed the cuddly canine to her friends.

Stephanie's reaction reminded Leslie of the way she had been approaching God lately — hesitant to open the packages He wanted to give her every day. God offers us so many gifts — the gift of grace, the gift of peace, the gift of talents and abilities, the gift of love, the gift of eternal life. But all too often we stand and stare at His packages and comment on how nice they are. We never accept the gifts as our own. We never open them to see what's inside.

Unopened, Stephanie's birthday present was just a pretty package. But when she accepted the present as her own and opened it, the package became a true gift from her mother's heart. With giggles and excited chatter, the girls disappeared to find the perfect spot in Stephanie's room for her newest stuffed toy. And at the same time, Leslie opened her heart to receive the present God had for her — a gaily-wrapped package that became a gift of joy from God's heart to hers.

Does God have a package waiting for you to open?

A joy that's shared is a joy made double.

UNKNOWN

SURVIVAL SKILLS

J ocelyn kept the food stamps hidden until all of her groceries had been rung up.

"That'll be $38.71," said the cashier.

Jocelyn's face turned red. She didn't look like the average person who used food stamps. She was dressed for an office job in a nice dress and heels. She felt people stare at her as though she'd done something wrong when she pulled out the food stamps. She quickly paid for her items, then hurried through the door. If she'd had her children with her, maybe people would have understood. Even though she had a job, she didn't have enough money to feed her family, and she felt ashamed.

That same year, she had needed emergency surgery for an ovarian cyst that kept doubling in size every two weeks. The doctors were afraid it was cancerous, while she was more afraid of the hospital bill. Explaining her dilemma to the doctor, she learned that the welfare system would cover her unexpected expenses.

The same week that Jocelyn needed surgery, one of her sons was hospitalized with what appeared to be spinal meningitis. The doctors refused to put off her

Trust in the Lord with all your heart and lean not on your own understanding; in all your ways submit to him and he will make your paths straight.

PROVERBS 3:5-6

surgery, and she ended up in a ward without even a telephone. With her eleven-year-old son in another hospital some fifteen miles away, she had never felt so alone. And because they were new to the area, there was no one to talk to, or visit, her young son — not even her.

"Lord, I'm all alone," Jocelyn prayed. "Please help me to talk to my son."

When she told her doctor about her situation, he had her moved to a semi-private room, where a phone waited beside her bed — all at the doctor's expense.

Are you in desperate need? Put your trust in your loving Father, and boldly ask Him for help. He will take care of you.

If we love Christ much, surely we shall
trust him much.

THOMAS BENTON BROOKS

KITCHEN-SINK LEGACY

> "Do to others as you would have them do to you."
>
> LUKE 6:31

Corinna's grandmother never went to seminary, but she sure could preach. From her kitchen-sink pulpit, Grandma would sermonize while she scrubbed the supper dishes. Her congregation of assembled relatives labored alongside her, clearing the table, drying the dishes, and putting away the pots and pans. Even the children were assigned after-dinner chores.

Corinna wanted to be like the neighbor children who gulped down their meals and left their dishes on the table as they flew out the back door to play. But Grandma would have none of that. If Corinna even hinted at wanting to be excused from her chores, Grandma would answer her with, "If you don't work, you don't eat." And then she would tell a story about how work wouldn't hurt her. By the time Grandma finished her sermonizing, it would be dark outside, and Corinna would have to wait until the next day to play with her friends. She quickly learned to do her chores without excuse or complaint; otherwise Grandma would remind her to "do everything without grumbling or complaining."

It seemed Grandma had a saying for every situation. If someone was upset about the treatment they had received from a friend, a clerk, or a neighbor, Grandma answered with, "Do to others as you would have them do to you." Or if she overheard one of the kids hinting that they were considering something naughty, Grandma quickly countered with, "Be sure your sin will find you out."

Only much later did Corinna discover that Grandma's gems of wisdom came from God's Word. Jesus' words to His disciples were Grandma's answer to bad manners. Paul's words to the Thessalonians and the Philippians were Grandma's encouragement for her to do her chores without complaint. And Moses' words to the wandering Israelites were Grandma's disapproval of wrongdoing.

Grandma's example demonstrates that everyday chores can be used as an opportunity to share God's love. Why not start a kitchen-sink legacy of your own and let your words—God's words—light the pathway for others?

We should behave to our friends as we
would wish our friends to behave to us.

ARISTOTLE

TENDING HIS FLOCK

> He tends his flock like a shepherd: He gathers the lambs in his arms and carries them close to his heart; he gently leads those that have young.
>
> ISAIAH 40:11

Eight-year-old Jonathan was always tempting fate. His mother often held her breath, watching him climb to the highest branches of a tall pine tree. Swaying in the breeze, he'd call down to her, "Hey, Mom, watch me!"

One day, Jonathan was riding his bike at breakneck speed downhill beside the house. At the bottom of the hill was his swing set, minus the swings. His mother watched in disbelief as her son raced down the hill, stood on the bicycle seat, then grabbed the top bar of the swing set.

She stifled a scream as he quickly flipped over the top of the bar and landed flat on his back on the cold, hard ground. It seemed to take forever for her to reach her son, who was uncharacteristically quiet. Gently, she lifted him in her arms, carried him back to the house.

Jonathan's chest ached, and he was breathing hard after having the breath knocked out of him. His mother wasted no time in dialing the doctor's office. While the pediatrician's phone rang, Jonathan said, "Mom, I'm not hurt. I'm all right."

She began checking him for any sign of injury. Looking over his arms and legs, she was surprised to see where Jonathan had circled, with a ballpoint pen, every hurt, scar, scrape, and bruise.

"What's all this?" she asked.

Jonathan sat up on the sofa, beaming. "That's all my hurts. I put a circle around all of them," he said. Within minutes, he'd forgotten all about his pain, and after a bowl of mint chocolate-chip ice cream, he ran outside again.

Like a loving mother, God gathers His children up in His arms time and again, carrying us close to His heart. We can find comfort that He knows all of our hurts. He knows the exact number of hairs on our heads, and our names are engraved on the palms of His hands. We may never know how many times God's providential hand has prevented an injury, either physical or emotional, in our lives. What a blessing to know He is ever tending His flock and protecting His lambs!

If God maintains sun and planets in
bright and ordered beauty, he can keep us.

F. B. MEYER

SEND IN THE CLOWNS

When the circus came to town, posters went up on the grocery store bulletin boards, billboards announced the performance dates, and television commercials urged listeners to "Come one; come all!" Lion tamers, wire walkers, and trapeze artists were part of the three-ring extravaganza. But the most anticipated performers were the clowns. With their crazy antics and outlandish costumes, they livened up each performance.

> Whatever you do, work at it with all your heart, as working for the Lord, not for human masters.
>
> COLOSSIANS 3:23

Clowns work hard at their profession. In fact, in order to travel with the Ringling Brothers Circus, clowns must successfully complete clown college — an intense course of study that covers everything from makeup to pratfalls, costuming to making balloon animals, juggling to sleight of hand. Only after clowns have mastered all of these skills can they take their place in the circus ring.

As Sheila stood at the stove sautéing vegetables for supper, she sensed a connection to this group of performers in the circus. Though she didn't wear a clown costume or clown makeup, she worked hard at juggling — balancing her time among home, family, work, friends, and church. She wasn't skilled at card tricks or sleight of hand, but she could work "magic," transforming everyday grocery items into flavorful meals seven days a week. And while she might not know the ins and outs of balloon-animal art, she made lots of other things, from costumes for school plays to crafty Christmas gifts and decorated birthday cakes. And she had taken many a fall — not pratfalls, but real falls — when she'd gone inline skating with the children or walked the dog on icy sidewalks.

God's Word says that we are to work at whatever we do with all our hearts, remembering that whatever we do is for the Lord. Whether we're clowns or cooks, minstrels or mothers, we need to work hard at our profession. And when we do, we might just provide our friends and families with some laughter along the way!

Lord, turn the routines of work into the
celebrations of love.

UNKNOWN

PERFECT LANDING

Betty was normally a pretty good cook. She could prepare some delicious meals for her family, as long as they didn't want anything too difficult. One day, however, her husband asked her to make biscuits for dinner. She had never attempted such a feat before, but with determination as her guide, she went to the grocery store to buy the ingredients. Luckily, there was a recipe on the flour bag. As she gathered all the ingredients, she dreamed of the lightest, fluffiest biscuits ever.

> She is clothed with strength and dignity; she can laugh at the days to come.
>
> PROVERBS 31:25

When she arrived home, she preheated the oven, placed the ingredients before her, and began the process of biscuit preparation. Everything seemed to be going fine, and soon she placed the baking dish in the oven. The biscuits even smelled great as they cooked. She was so excited that she called her starving family to dinner before she removed the biscuits from the oven. All the chattering kids sat down and placed their napkins in their laps. While she stirred the stew, she asked her husband to take the pan out of the oven and place it on the table.

Then everything got quiet. The kids looked at one another in disbelief, as their father shushed them with a glance. He followed his wife's instructions and placed the pan of biscuits on the hot pad. With an expectant smile on her face, Betty turned around to look. No one else was smiling. The biscuits were as flat as pancakes. Her family's eyes focused on her, waiting for an explosion of tears. Instead, Betty reached down and picked up a biscuit to examine it.

"What's that, Mom?" her youngest daughter asked.

"A Frisbee!" she shouted, and she sailed the biscuit across the room. Laughter broke the tense silence. The biscuits may have not been perfect, but the atmosphere was a joyful one as Betty's family enjoyed their mother's spontaneity.

The ability to turn a disaster into a comical situation is one we could all learn. There's enough in life to be serious about, so learn to laugh as often as you can!

Laughter is the joyous universal
evergreen of life.

ABRAHAM LINCOLN

KITCHEN SABOTAGE!

God is not a God of disorder but of peace.

1 CORINTHIANS 14:33

Kathleen's kitchen cupboards and drawers were a mess. Cupboards overflowed with mismatched dishes, receipts, expired prescriptions, and nearly empty bottles of cough medicine. Plastic storage dishes and lids seemed to be multiplying in the bottom drawer. Trying to find a wooden spoon in the drawer next to the stove was like going on a treasure hunt. And odds and ends of twist ties, clothespins, and rubber bands cluttered the silverware drawer. There was no doubt about it. Her kitchen had been sabotaged by the excesses of daily life!

When her husband announced an upcoming camping trip, Kathleen sensed an opportunity to undo some of the damage to the kitchen. She helped pack food, swimming supplies, sleeping bags, flashlights, toys, and the clothes needed for a weekend in the woods. But when the time came for the car and camper to pull out of the driveway, she was not aboard. Her husband and daughter headed off for a weekend of fun and frolic while she turned back to the house to face the kitchen clutter monster!

Armed with cleaning supplies, trash bags, and new shelf paper, Kathleen surveyed the kitchen and mapped out her strategy. Soon she had unloaded the contents of the cupboards onto the kitchen table, the hallway floor, and the living room furniture. Time flew by, and she barely stopped to eat. But the interiors of those cupboards smelled fresh and clean, and the only items allowed back were things that were supposed to be there. Then she tackled the drawers.

When Kathleen tumbled into bed well past midnight, the cupboards were done. The drawers were organized. The counters were clear. Her body ached, but it felt good. She had taken a disorganized mess and made it into a useful kitchen once again. Now maybe she could find some time to spend with God.

Is there an area of your home or life that has been sabotaged by the excesses of life? Look for ways to set those things in order. The sense of accomplishment that accompanies your labor may even invigorate you for greater tasks!

Our life is frittered away by detail . . .
simplify, simplify.

HENRY DAVID THOREAU

PENNY BEAR

I n the 1950s, a honey distributor packaged its honey in a glass bottle shaped like a baby bear. Grandma used this brand of honey in her cooking, and she quickly used up the contents of the uniquely shaped bottle. The bottle was too pretty to throw away, so she put the bottle to use as a penny jar. Whenever she found a penny on the sidewalk or received a penny in change, she would place those small copper coins in the bear-shaped bottle on her kitchen counter.

> They will lay up treasure for themselves as a firm foundation for the coming age.
>
> 1 TIMOTHY 6:19

Her grandchildren loved to count the pennies in Grandma's "penny bear." They'd pour the penny bear's contents onto the kitchen table and make neat stacks of pennies. Then they'd write the date and the total amount of pennies on a small slip of paper and tuck it into the penny bear's lid. Whenever the penny bear was full, Grandma took it to the bank and put the pennies in a savings account. The empty penny bear reappeared on the kitchen counter with a clean slip of paper in its lid. And so the process continued year after year.

When her oldest granddaughter began preparations for college, Grandma said she had something to give her. As she entered Grandma's kitchen, her granddaughter noticed a piece of paper sticking out of the top of the empty penny bear. She picked up the bottle and discovered that the paper was a check for the total cost of her books for her first semester at college. Because of Grandma's penny-saving habits, there was enough money in the penny bear account to buy her college textbooks for that first semester and for several more years.

Now whenever her granddaughter finds a penny on the ground, she thanks God for Grandma's faithful stewardship. One penny is not worth much. But one penny multiplied can feed a hungry family, house a homeless person, or help a child through college. Little things do mean a lot.

Whoever is capable of giving is rich.

ERICH FROMM

VOLCANO STEW

Tina was running late again, and by the time she had climbed into her car in the parking lot, the streets were already clogged with rush-hour traffic. The leisurely, mid-morning, ten-minute drive home became a stoplight-ridden, horn-honking, thirty-minute commute.

> Rejoice in the Lord always. I will say it again: Rejoice!
>
> PHILIPPIANS 4:4

She finally stumbled into the house muttering apologies and grabbed the pot of leftover stew from the refrigerator. Slamming it on the stove, she flipped on the burner and rushed to change into some comfortable clothes while hollering, "Someone please set the table!"

A few minutes later when she rushed back into the kitchen, her nose sensed disaster. The stove! The pot of stew she had placed on the burner was a bubbling imitation of Mount Vesuvius. Tall columns of tomato-red sauce spurted into the air above the pot. Pieces of vegetables spewed over its sides. Apparently, in her haste to start supper, she had turned the burner to its highest setting, and now the stew was erupting all over the stovetop.

Tina shrieked, and her family hurried into the kitchen. The pot was boiling so furiously that it was impossible to turn the burner off without being spattered by the tomato-sauce columns. The foaming vegetables were spilling over so quickly that no one could grab the pot's handles without getting burned. But someone had to try. Amid exclamations of "Ouch!" "Hey, that's hot!" and "Yeow!" hands reached from all directions and eased the pot from its heat source.

Quickly Tina switched the burner off and surveyed the kitchen. Stew was splattered everywhere, and everyone's hands were covered with the sticky red goo. Her oldest child broke the silence. With a glint in her eye, she licked the stew from her hands and said, "Good dinner, Mom."

The laughter that accompanied the cleanup that night echoed with the Bible's admonition to always rejoice. If we have God's perspective on life, we can rejoice in everything — even volcano stew.

A good laugh is sunshine in a house.

PHILLIP JAMES BAILEY

TEENAGE TRAUMA

"But, Mom, all the girls are wearing black lipstick!" her teenage daughter cried.

"I don't care if they're wearing blue lipstick," Carol screamed. "You are not going out of this house dressed like a witch!"

Rachel stomped her foot and flounced out of the kitchen, and Carol winced as she heard her daughter slam the bedroom door. First it was miniskirts and a pierced nose, and now this. She fumed as she slapped mustard on a ham sandwich to take for lunch. What on earth was she going to do about that girl?

Remember when you wore miniskirts and white go-go boots? the still, small voice of God reminded her. *Remember pale pink lipstick and bare midriffs?*

Yes, Lord, she argued inside, *but You don't approve of her rebellion, do You?*

God seemed to answer, *I loved you even when you were yet in sin.*

Carol *did* love her daughter, despite Rachel's outrageous behavior . . . and she had to admit, she had done

Charm can be deceptive and beauty doesn't last, but a woman who fears and reverences God shall be greatly praised.

PROVERBS 31:30 TLB

some pretty stupid things when she was a teenager.

Carol sighed. She didn't want to drive her daughter away like her own mother had done to her.

"Rachel," she said, tapping at the door. "Can we talk?"

"Go away!" her daughter sobbed.

"Please?" Gently, Carol opened the door and sat down on the bed beside her daughter. "I love you, you know. That's why I care so much."

Rachel rolled away from her mother and said, "All you care about is what your friends will say!"

"Right now, all I care about is what you have to say. Talk to me."

Every teenager is unique and special, yet every teenager needs the same things: love, discipline, and understanding. Start a dialogue with your teenager today.

The first duty of love is to listen.

PAUL TILLICH

LET'S TRY IT AGAIN!

Misty held her big brother's hand in a vise-like grip. Her eyes widened as she took in the incredible scene playing out before her. There, atop the best sledding hill in all of Connecticut, her eighty-year-old grandmother was preparing for the ride of her life.

> A heart at peace gives life to the body.
>
> PROVERBS 14:30

Poised on the toboggan, she sat as royalty, her long fur coat wrapped around her legs and her fur cap pinned perfectly into place. A small push on the snow with her elegant gloved hand . . . and she was off.

Halfway down the hill, the toboggan toppled to the side, and Misty watched in horror as her grandmother did an amazing acrobatic move through the snow, tumbling three times before sliding to a halt midway. Running full tilt to the rescue, Misty arrived breathless before a disheveled lump of fur.

Rosy cheeks appeared beneath a fur cap that was relocated to cover one ear. Snow was encrusted in the hair surrounding her face, and her bright, mischievous eyes met Misty's fearful gaze. With the confident laugh of one who loves God and knows of His care, Grandmother grabbed hold of Misty's hand and said, "Again! Let's try it again!"

That afternoon outing—followed by laughter and steaming mugs of hot chocolate around the kitchen table — made for one memorable winter day!

Whether it's an attempt at sledding for the first time in eighty years, or taking the hand of one you love and risking the exposure of your heart, God offers you the peace that brings comfort in the midst of life's chaos. In fact, it gives Him great pleasure. If you ask, God will give you the confidence to step into life's adventures, knowing that His hand will always be there to catch you.

Confidence in the natural world is self-reliance, in the spiritual world it is God-reliance.

OSWALD CHAMBERS

REALISTIC EXPECTATIONS

"Watch out! Can't you be more careful?" It seemed lately like Jackie had been saying those words far too often to her six-year-old, Katie. This time her daughter's love of ketchup had resulted in a large tomato stain on a brand-new tablecloth. It had been a long day already, and Jackie's temper flared as the angry words escaped her lips. But as the words tumbled out, she saw Katie's quivering lip and a tear slip out of the corner of her eye.

> The Lord has compassion on those who fear him; for he knows how we are formed.
>
> PSALMS 103:13-14

Jackie felt terrible. Sure, the bottle had fallen over, but her daughter had not intentionally made a mountain of ketchup on the table. It was an accident. Jackie had responded inappropriately and barked an angry response without thinking.

She stopped wiping the stain and reached across the table to give her child a hug. And then she looked her straight in the eye and said, "I'm sorry I yelled at you. Will you forgive Mommy?"

Her daughter's tear-stained face nodded a reply, and they sat locked in a soggy embrace for several seconds.

Later, while finishing the dishes, Jackie thought again of the ketchup incident. And she thought about how much her daughter had changed since she was a baby.

Katie could run, play, read, color, sing, and laugh now; and Jackie expected so much from her at times. As Katie matured, her mother forgot too easily that she was only six years old. She often expected her to behave as if she were nine or ten.

Thankfully, God isn't like that. Yes, He has expectations for us. But God knows us and knows our needs. He readily forgives us when we get angry or do something wrong. He provides the things we need when we need them. He restores broken relationships and grants us wisdom and direction for living. But best of all, God remembers how He made us. And in His compassion, He never expects more from us than what He knows we can do or be.

Have a heart that never hardens, a temper that never tires, and a touch that never hurts.

CHARLES DICKENS

PEACE AT LAST

With a throbbing headache, Diane prepared breakfast for her children and made a mental note of all the people she needed to contact. Her aunt in the nursing home would love to have her stop by for a chat, as would her single neighbor down the street. But she just didn't have the time! Diane pushed the boxed greeting cards out of the way to set down the cereal bowls, and she thought of a friend who had just lost her mother. A simple card could say so much.

Her thoughts were interrupted by the telephone. Her prayer partner told her that a man in their church had just suffered a heart attack. So many needs, and so little time!

"If only I had time to take care of all these things, Lord," she whispered, just as her kids ran into the kitchen arguing with one another.

In a few minutes, the kids were gone, and silence filled the house. Finally, she could rest. She turned on the television, then it dawned on her that this would be the perfect time to address a few cards and make some calls. She picked up the greeting cards and wrote down her

"Peace I leave with you; my peace I give you. I do not give to you as the world gives. Do not let your hearts be troubled and do not be afraid."

JOHN 14:27

thoughts. After addressing the envelopes, she picked up the phone and called the heart-attack victim's wife. The report was good.

After a few minutes of prayer, Diane took a shower and realized that her headache had disappeared. She dropped her cards in the mailbox and briefly visited her aunt, who gave her a much-needed hug. Then she returned home and had the entire afternoon to clean house and prepare dinner. After dinner there was enough left over to take a plateful of food to a lonely neighbor.

When she got home, Diane thought she had never felt better. God had given her the time she needed to take care of all the things that had weighed so heavily on her heart. And in giving, she had received far more than she ever expected.

At times, peace comes when we least expect it. But often, if we take notice, we'll realize that peace follows closely on the heels of reaching out to others.

God takes life's pieces and gives us
unbroken peace.

W. D. GOUGH

SPIRITUAL PHYSICS

"**M**ama!" Josh's voice carried through the quiet house.

"Yes, Josh?"

"Mama! Come bounce me!"

> He who walks with the wise grows wise.
>
> PROVERBS 13:20

Mary looked out the kitchen window to the trampoline that seemed to take up half the yard. With a smile that dimpled her cheeks, she grasped her youngest son's hand and went out to bounce him. It was an odd sort of pride she took in being able to skyrocket her son's little body into the air. She outweighed him by a number of pounds, and her weight caused him to go higher than any of his friends could take him. It was just a simple matter of physics, really; the heavier your partner, the higher you go.

It's no different spiritually. The people you surround yourself with will either send you skyrocketing into spiritual understanding and maturity or leave you grounded and struggling.

When you look at those in your life today, who is it that stands out as wise? Who walks with that quiet charisma and peace that you find yourself craving? What would it take to call that person? Keep it simple and comfortable. Plan a casual lunch at home, invite her over for coffee, or simply spend an afternoon talking. Or perhaps you can find an activity you both enjoy. Surround yourself with people who will encourage your spiritual growth.

The Bible says in James 1:5, "If any of you lacks wisdom, he should ask God." Ask God to expand your wisdom and your world.

Wisdom is seeing life from God's
perspective.

BILL GOTHARD

HIDE AND SEEK

Then Barnabas went to Tarsus to look for Saul.

ACTS 11:25

When Lucille's children were young, they enjoyed playing hide and seek in the dark. The old country kitchen with its cavernous cupboards and deep recesses contained many good places to hide. On one such occasion, one of their cousins —the smallest one, in fact—curled up into the back of the cupboard where Lucille kept her baking pans. When the pans were moved close to the cupboard door, the child was virtually invisible behind them. It was an ideal hiding place.

With a shout of "Ready or not, here I come!" the game started. One by one, the hiding places and hidden children were found. But the littlest cousin, curled up in the baking pan cupboard, evaded discovery. An older child would have been thrilled at not being found. But this child didn't see things that way. Sipping a cup of tea in the darkened kitchen, Lucille heard a tiny voice whimper, "Isn't anyone going to come looking for me?" That little voice was all it took for the rest of the children to locate their cousin. Though the others congratulated him on his hiding place, he was just glad someone had found him.

Though Paul wasn't playing hide and seek, the Bible tells us that he had been hidden in Tarsus for quite some time. He could have easily felt abandoned by the other believers. He could have wondered if anyone even cared to know where he was. But then God sent Barnabas to find Paul. And when Barnabas found him, the two of them began a missionary journey that would ultimately change their world for Christ.

Though we may not play hide and seek anymore as grown-ups, we can sometimes feel buried under responsibilities and schedules that close in on us and hide us from time with friends and family. That's when we need someone like Barnabas—someone to seek us out and show us that they care.

Do you know someone who needs a Barnabas? Reach out—with a note, a phone call, a prayer, or a visit—and do a little seeking, not hiding, today.

Kindness in words creates confidence.
Kindness in thinking creates
profoundness. Kindness in giving creates
love.

LAO-TSE

CARDINAL GRACE

While her six-year-old granddaughter fought the cancer that had invaded her brain, Donna often was amazed at Jennifer's childlike faith. Jenny had no doubt that God loved her and watched over her. Donna always accompanied her daughter and Jennifer to the hospital for the chemotherapy treatments, and when they returned home, they would always stop in the city park for a few minutes. Even though the treatments made her nauseated, Jennifer wanted to drive the long way home to see the beautiful spring flowers, but she especially liked to watch the robins, blue jays, and cardinals. The cardinals were her favorite, she said, because red was her favorite color.

After her last treatment, the doctor confirmed what they feared most of all. She only had a short time to live. When she was not in a drug-induced sleep, she would tell her grandmother about the cardinal that frequently perched on her windowsill. No one but Jenny ever saw it.

Several months after Jenny passed away, Donna stood crying at her sink, feeling as cold and barren as the winter

> Give me a sign of your goodness, that my enemies may see it and be put to shame, for you, Lord, have helped me and comforted me.
>
> PSALM 86:17

landscape. Her grief clung to her like a shroud. Why God? she cried as she had so many other times. Just then, a flash of red startled her. A cardinal! Fascinated, Donna watched as the most beautiful cardinal she had ever seen perched on the kitchen windowsill and cocked its head at her. Her tears stopped, replaced by the warmth and assurance of God's love. A moment later, the cardinal took flight and disappeared.

For days, the cardinal visited her every morning, and she found her heart growing lighter. Every day brought a cherished memory of Jenny's laughter, and Donna knew without a doubt that her granddaughter was happy and greatly loved by God. And she knew that one day, she would see her again.

Are you mourning the loss of a loved one? God wants you to know that He loves you and He sees your tears. Let Him comfort you today.

God is closest to those whose hearts are broken.

JEWISH PROVERB

DO YOU PROMISE?

S amantha had to have the promise. Every night at bedtime, she always called out to her mother as she walked away from her closed bedroom door: "Mom? Do you promise?"

"Yes, Honey, I promise."

> The Lord is my light and my salvation —whom shall I fear?
>
> PSALM 27:1

Every night, she and her mother said the same words. Their ritual began with Samantha's fear of tornadoes, then dogs, then the green-eyed slime monster that she had glimpsed on a television show she wasn't supposed to be watching. Fear of snakes, the boogeyman, thunderstorms, fire ants (her mother is still not sure what brought that one on!), winged creatures of every sort, and fires followed one after another.

But later, the promise was no longer specific . . . just the general promise that Sam would wake up whole, unscathed by alien dream creatures, and free from wounds inflicted by nature.

Her mother took a risk every night, promising that no harm would come to her young daughter. The truth was, a thunderstorm could occur, a fire ant could crawl into her bed, and even a tornado was not beyond the realm of possibility.

But in another sense, there was no risk. The Bible says that there is no fear in Christ Jesus. He is the snake Killer, the thunderstorm Tamer, and the Water that douses every fire. He annihilates the boogeyman, and there is no winged creature that could escape His wrath. With God on your side, there is absolutely nothing to fear! It's tough to fathom but so important to grasp. When your heart rests with Him, there is no one who can break it. When your aching body cries for help, He is there to grant you peace. Even in the face of death, He brings life to the darkness. There is no caging His protective presence. Cast off your fear; He will take it and tame it. For *His* promises can never be broken!

The wise man in the storm prays to God, not for safety from danger, but for deliverance from fear. It is the storm within which endangers him, not the storm without.

RALPH WALDO EMERSON

A SOOTHING LOTION

Anne felt bloated. The pain from her incision was excruciating, worsened by the hacking cough she could not seem to shake. Her husband was at work, and her new daughter was sleeping soundly in her crib. In the moment of silence, she tried to absorb the peace that seemed to surround her but remained far from her grasp.

Anne's mother sat beside her, her dark brown eyes comforting and understanding as she read the restlessness and frustration in her daughter's face. Anne had been home from the hospital for just forty-eight hours, yet her doctor had prescribed six weeks of recovery time after the emergency caesarean section. Anne struggled not to feel sorry for herself. It was difficult, though. Her distant husband seemed cold and uncaring; her home was in a shambles; and her pain was unbearable.

Anne continued to wallow in her misery and barely noticed as her mother knelt before her and gently removed the socks from her swollen, hurting feet. Her mother took one foot in her hands and began to rub it in a smooth, rhythmic motion. The pain lessened.

As Anne watched her mother's aging hands soothing her swollen ankles, applying lotion to the dry areas, and massaging the calluses, she marveled. Her mother's hands were strong and tenacious, characteristic of a woman who had held her own in every aspect of life. Anne glanced down at her own tender hands. They were still plump with youth—full and unlined. They didn't have the marks of wisdom, the edges of strength, or the grasp of one who labors. She realized that the one she should serve was serving her.

Just like Jesus washed the feet of His disciples before the Last Supper, God serves us, comforts us, and holds us in His arms in the midst of confusion. He assures us through His Word that He will be there to comfort us in the midst of life's chaos, even more than a mother comforts her own child. Rest in that knowledge today. Let it be a soothing lotion to the dry and barren patches of your soul.

God does not comfort us to make us comfortable, but to make us comforters.

JOHN HENRY JOWETT

PLAYFUL JOY

Grandma Lu watched her grandson, a bit perplexed by his actions. Benjamin, in all his six-year-old glory, was spinning. Not for any apparent reason, he was simply spinning, around and around and around. His little arms were stretched out on either side of his body, and his head was thrown back as a deep belly laugh escaped from his rosy lips. It didn't seem that he was doing much . . . hardly anything amusing or interesting. Grandma Lu paused.

> [There is] a time to weep and a time to laugh.
>
> ECCLESIASTES 3:4

Was there something fun about spinning? she wondered. She glanced around the lobby of the hotel where she sat. There were only a few people nearby, and they were buried deep in magazines and newspapers. She stood up and set her purse on the seat, blushing even as she walked toward her spinning grandson. She wasn't sure if there was any special technique, so she watched him for a moment before spreading out her own arms. She began slowly at first, careful not to bump into anything, worried she might slip and fall. Then she threw caution to the wind and began to speed up. She threw her head back and laughed, as she felt the momentum of her own body carry her in circles. What fun!

A few minutes later, she slowed to a stop. Benjamin stood before her, his mouth open, his eyes wide. He began to laugh, and she laughed with him. They made quite a pair in that hotel lobby — disheveled, flushed, spinning grandmother and grandson. But people smiled because their joy was real.

Laughter is God's gift of healing for a saddened heart. It gives lightness to the spirit and gets the blood flowing. Find a way to laugh today: rent a funny movie, read the comics, or play with a child and forget you're an adult. Do things you wouldn't normally think of doing and allow yourself to enjoy them. There is a time to laugh. Take that time today, and revel in the abandonment of playful joy.

Laughing is the sensation of feeling good all over and showing it principally in one spot.

JOSH BILLINGS

MONSTER HUGS

"That's thirty-four monster hugs, Mommy!" Sandy said as she tugged on her mother's shirt and pointed to the chart on the refrigerator. "Yup! Since I did my room, that's three, and then I was nice to our guests, that's five . . . and then I get an extra five for being your favorite daughter!"

"You're my only daughter, Sandy!" her mom laughed.

"Yes, but that should be worth at least five!"

Sandy smiled at her mother in that mischievous way and wrote "34" at the far end of the chart. Her mother didn't stop her. Why begrudge her five monster hugs? They were a pleasure to give. She picked up her daughter, who at age seven was getting harder to lift, dropped her on the couch, and kissed, giggled, and cuddled — each monster hug lasting about thirty seconds. Every time her daughter did something well, she earned monster hugs. Not only were they a pleasure for Sandy, but they also were a joy for her mother, an incentive that tied their love together.

> Our mouths were filled with laughter, our tongues with songs of joy.
>
> PSALM 126:2

How much more does our Father in Heaven wish to reward us for steps in the right direction! It is as much a pleasure for Him to give as it is for us to receive. He enjoys blessing us. He knows our greatest pleasures and our deepest desires, and as we remain faithful, He, like a loving father, envisions the fun He will have in giving us our reward.

Even when it seems difficult, even when the task is hard, stay faithful. Right now, your Father is planning for the best monster hugs ever, with you as the giggling recipient.

Laughter is the music of life.

SIR WILLIAM OSLER

REVOLVING DOOR

A imee felt like her life was caught in a revolving door. Each day seemed like the day before, with no way out of the routine. She pulled herself out of bed each morning and headed to the kitchen to brew that necessary pick-me-up called coffee. After preparing lunches and cooking breakfast, she dropped the kids off at school and battled traffic on the way to work. By the time she reached her office, it felt as though she had already done a day's work.

> "Come to me, all you who are weary and burdened, and I will give you rest."
>
> MATTHEW 11:28

Once she arrived at her desk, she had telephone calls to return and a mountain of paperwork to tackle. Problems crowded out the pleasure her career was supposed to bring. Trapped in that revolving door, she just went around and around, doing the same things day after day.

Dinner was just as much of a routine as the rest of her life. *What will it be tonight?* she wondered. *Chicken, pork, or beef? If it's Tuesday, then it must be beef.* Even the revolving schedule of food preparation kept her in the same rut. Exhaustion set in as she piled pots and pans into the sink after dinner. She had to find a better way of getting through the day! Aimee realized that the only thing she could change was her attitude.

The next morning when she woke, she prayed first—

the first step out of that revolving door. She kissed and hugged her children, sang in the shower, dressed, and hurried to her car, slowing down for a moment to notice the flowers in bloom. When she got to the office, she thanked God for the opportunity to work for such a good company. The revolving door began slowing down. That night, she transformed the same old beef into beef stroganoff and the dishwashing into a family affair. The kids had never seen her this way, and they didn't want to miss a minute of it.

If your life is stuck in a revolving door, step out and enjoy the peace that God offers. He'll be with you all along the way as you pray, sing, and change your tune.

———————————

True peace is found by man in the depths of his own heart, the dwelling-place of God.

JOHANN TAULER

THE HAND OF FRIENDSHIP

It's not always easy to love. Growing up, Ben and Mary constantly fought. As brother and sister, they were inseparable, but they were interested only in tormenting each other—a push here, a shove there, stolen cookies, disappearing toys.

> "This is my command: love each other."
>
> JOHN 15:17

One spring afternoon, their mother reached her limit. She sat down both her young children and looked from one to the other. "I've had enough of your fighting. For the rest of the day, I don't want to hear a single raised voice, a thud from hitting one another, a scream, or a cry. I want you to play nicely, love each other, and be kind. Period. End of story. Just do it." She got up, brushed herself off, and went back to her tasks, unable to do or say anymore.

Ben and Mary sat and looked at each other. Love each other? How could they love each other? Just by being told? Especially when the sight of the other was enough to bring mud bombs and hair-pulling to mind? But they had never seen their mother quite so angry.

A few moments passed in silence until Ben finally reached out, took Mary's hand, and asked, "Want to build a fort?"

Mary smiled and said, "Okay."

Of course, it's not always quite as easy as grabbing someone's hand and playing soldier, but it's also not as hard as we might think. Sometimes loving each other is simply a matter of letting go, starting anew with a fresh page before you, and deciding that the past is gone and all you have is the future to mold. It's a matter of extending your hand in friendship and choosing to play rather than argue.

God commands us to love one another. Can you think of someone you have refused to love? Is there something you can do to extend a hand of friendship? Even if it is rejected, God asks only that you do your part. He will see to the rest. You never know; it may work out better than you imagine. The person might even say, "Okay!"

Love is most divine when it loves according to needs, and not according to merit.

GEORGE MACDONALD

ADOPTED FOR LIFE

Some years ago, Jack brought Susie home from a "foster home" because his wife wanted a basset hound. Instead of the beautiful tri-colored animal she expected, Susie was the color of red Georgia clay and something less than beautiful.

At first, Helen wanted to return the dog. It really didn't suit her tastes. Susie wasn't a show dog; she had no pedigree; and from what the woman could see, she wasn't even very special. After a week, however, she and the dog bonded.

Susie became a protective member of the family, barking at strangers and routinely following Helen's children to school. And as the years passed, Susie developed quite a character.

One time, Helen received a desperate phone call from a boy in her old neighborhood. She could hear the pain in his voice as he said, "You need to come over right away. Susie's not moving." Fearing the worst, she and her older boys drove down the street.

For he chose us in him before the creation of the world to be holy and blameless in his sight. In love he predestined us for adoption to sonship through Jesus Christ, in accordance with his pleasure and will . . .

EPHESIANS 1:4-5

Susie's still form was lying in the crabgrass. Helen leaned out the window and called to her. The animal didn't move. She opened the car door and walked slowly toward the motionless body. She saw one lazy ear perk up. "Thank goodness," she whispered, "she's still alive!"

Just as Helen leaned down to see how badly she was hurt, Susie jumped up and gave her the sloppiest dog kiss ever. Throwing her arms around the dog, she realized Susie was as much a part of her family as any of her children.

When we are adopted into the family of God, we are no longer a part of the world's family; we are part of a Heavenly family that serves a sovereign Lord. What a blessing to be His child!

The love we give away is the only love we keep.

ELBERT HUBBARD

A BUBBLY CHALLENGE

Sometimes, being a mother is simply not easy. One dreary winter day, Barbara, the mother of two toddlers, felt discouraged as she swept up cookie crumbs and wiped up spilled juice. She was exhausted from trying to prevent her two little ones from getting into one thing after another.

> Like arrows in the hands of a warrior are sons born in one's youth. Bless is the man whose quiver is full of them.
>
> PSALMS 127:4-5

While she answered the doorbell, her daughter slipped into a white eyelet dress to parade around the kitchen in bare feet. Barbara picked up her unhappy child and marched her into the bedroom to change.

After putting shoes on the children, she planned a trip to the store. Setting both of her toddlers in front of the television for a moment, she went into her bedroom to get ready. Before she could zip her jeans, she heard an earsplitting shriek from outside. She dashed out the back door and caught her daughter innocently letting the cat out of the cooler.

"What was that cat doing in there?" she asked.

Before her daughter could answer, she heard her three-year-old son squalling. He was lying face down on the other side of a three-foot high brick wall. Through his tears, he said, "Sissy pushed me." Barbara half-believed Sissy had put the cat in the cooler so there'd be no witnesses.

After fussing at her children for their disobedience, the woman felt a tug at her angry heart. "Please, Lord," she prayed, "give me peace and patience with my children."

Later that evening, as the kids were taking their bath, Barbara heard giggling and laughing, so she peeked in on her little "angels." To her dismay, the room was filled with bubbles. Not a bit of bubble bath was left. Then she discovered that her bottle of peach- scented shampoo — her favorite — was completely empty. But the impatience she had felt earlier that day was replaced by a joyful, laughing heart.

Our ability to see our children as a blessing from God is sometimes a challenge. That's when we need to think as a child and discover how much fun is tucked away in a bottle of sweet-smelling shampoo.

Children need love, especially when they
don't deserve it.

HAROLD S. HULBERT

SEEDS OF CARE

As Jennifer eased the batter-dipped, sliced green tomatoes into the frying pan, the aroma brought back vivid memories. The snapshots in her mind were sharp and clear as she remembered her mother marrying the man from Alabama. Jennifer had been a teenager from the city, and she couldn't stand this man from the "sticks." To her, he was nothing but a country bumpkin.

> "A new command I give you: love one another. As I have loved you, so you must love one another."
>
> JOHN 13:34

Early one spring morning, everything changed. She was sitting on the backyard swing, watching as he turned the soil with a shovel on a sunny spot behind the house. Each day, he did something different: he'd break up dirt clods, toss rocks out, and add compost, finally raking the soil smooth. Curious, Jennifer walked across the garden, feeling the coolness of the newly worked earth between her toes.

"Here," said her stepfather, "take these." He poured some seeds into her open hand.

"What are they?" she asked, feeling her resentment dissipate in the cool morning.

"Squash," he said. "Later, I'll plant pole beans and tomatoes."

She watched that day as he planted the seeds, covering them with dirt and patting it down. Following his example, she soon completed a row of little mounds.

Later that summer, she enjoyed looking under the leaves of the squash plants and plucking the golden vegetables. She also liked the taste of a young cucumber, but most of all, she loved the green tomatoes her stepfather taught her to fry.

Jennifer smiled at the memory and at her eleven-year-old son, Jon, who waited patiently for the fried green tomatoes to cool. What her stepfather had done that day was to crumble the wall between them, much like he'd broken up the soil. Looking at her son, she knew that same love would continue for yet another generation.

Are you sowing seeds of love? Or are your seeds falling onto hard soil? Take the time to nurture and care for your "seeds." Break up the hard ground of resentment, and allow God to cause your love to grow in someone's heart.[29]

Love, that all gentle hearts so quickly
know.

DANTE ALIGHIERI

GIVING THANKS

The Thanksgiving table stood ready, a plump turkey in the center and a myriad of side dishes that seemed to cover every remaining square inch. The aroma of stuffing wafted from the oven door as Susan set out the deviled eggs.

The combined smells brought back the first Thanksgiving that Susan could remember. She had been a five-year-old then. That year she had contracted strep throat, which developed into rheumatic fever. She was sick for days. Her mother handled the sickness matter-of-factly, although she probably knew the risk of heart damage. Throughout the day and night, Susan would hear her mother slip into her room to check on her.

After the danger passed, Susan went to the doctor and learned that for the next year, she would not be allowed to run, exercise, or even walk fast, in order to prevent heart damage. That fall, as brightly colored leaves skittered to the ground, she walked slowly to and from school.

November arrived, and her kindergarten teacher prepared a Thanksgiving skit. Susan was excited as she dreamed of becoming one of the Indians who danced around the stage. But instead, she was told she would have to play the part of an oak tree. It was disappointing, but her mother taught her to be thankful anyway. At least she was part of the play.

Standing at the stove, Susan stirred the gravy. Other Thanksgivings came to mind—seasons when she'd lost loved ones. Although those were the hardest, she was thankful that God had blessed her with people who had made a difference in her life. And a smile graced her lips when she thought of the Thanksgivings when her children were toddlers. She could almost hear the kids sitting on the floor banging on pots and pans with wooden spoons.

Susan brought her mind back to the present as her family began arriving. Her grandchildren burst through the back door, and she hugged each one. And looking Heavenward, she thanked God for all the memories yet to be made.

Thanksgiving . . . invites God to bestow a second benefit.

ROBERT HERRICK

PRAYER FOR HARRIED MOMS

Financial hardship had forced Valerie to take a part-time job delivering newspapers. The route took two hours, and she had to bring her two young children along with her. After sitting at the kitchen table stuffing papers in plastic bags, Valerie started out with her two toddlers, a box of crackers, two apples, building blocks, a purple dinosaur, extra diapers, and seven stacks of newspapers.

> "He will take great delight in you; in his love he will no longer rebuke you, but will rejoice over you with singing."
>
> ZEPHANIAH 3:17

While she had gotten used to dodging large trucks, commercial buses, and a herd of goats, she was not used to her daughter repeatedly asking, "Mom, what can I eat?"

"Eat an apple," Valerie answered.

From the back seat came the reply, "They're all gone." The distraction threw Valerie off, and she missed a mailbox. She backed up and stuffed a paper in.

"Then eat a cracker," she said, biting her lip. Turning around, Valerie saw half the box of crackers littering the back seat. She groaned and said, "Amy, hand me a newspaper."

Halfway through the paper route and in the middle of nowhere, Amy started whining. "What's wrong, sweetheart?" Valerie asked.

"I've got to go to the bathroom."

Valerie gritted her teeth and pleaded, "Hold it."

"I can't!" Amy wailed.

Valerie turned the car around and headed for the nearest fast-food restaurant, but it was too late, and she reluctantly headed home for a change of clothes. With only forty minutes left, Valerie and her helpers arrived back on the paper route. Just as she stuffed the last paper in a box, she heard a hissing sound and stopped the car. Looking at the flat tire, she cried, "Lord, are You there?

Just about then, she heard singing coming from the back seat. "Jesus loves me, this I know . . ."

The Lord does love us. He loves us whether we're about to scream in exasperation or ready to shout for joy from a rooftop. When we know God is in ultimate control of everything, we can turn our circumstances over to Him and feel His love surround us.

How things look on the outside of us
depends on how things are on the inside
of us.

PARKS COUSINS

WALKING THROUGH
THE PAIN

He has
delivered
me from
all my
troubles.

PSALM 54:7

"Yes, you're going to the doctor's office," Jean said. "That's the only way you can be on the basketball team."

"But, Mom," whined Jamie. "I hate doctors! Maybe I'll just lay out of basketball this year." Her teenage daughter leaned back in the kitchen chair.

"Don't be silly," Jean said and motioned for her daughter to follow her to the car. "Basketball tryouts are in three weeks, and you have to take a physical." "Now hurry up, or we'll be late." Dragging her feet, Jamie crawled into the car and fastened her seat belt.

"They won't hurt me, will they, Mom?" Jamie asked in a small voice.

"Of course not."

Inside the waiting room, Jamie fidgeted as she sat on the wooden stool waiting for the nurse. After what seemed like hours, the nurse first checked her height and weight and then requested that she do a series of jumping jacks. Jamie grimaced at her mother and began jumping. The nurse checked her pulse rate. After Jamie's breathing returned to normal, the nurse asked, "Are you ready for the finger stick?"

With a look of betrayal, Jamie glared at her mother. "Will it hurt?" she asked.

"A little," the nurse said. She grasped Jamie's middle finger and quickly pricked it.

"That hurt!" Jamie hollered, examining the damage.

"You know," her mother said, trying to distract her daughter, "when I was pregnant, I had to have a finger stick every six weeks."

The teen's blue eyes twinkled, and a little smile played along her lips as she said, "You don't have to worry, Mom. The way I hate pain, I'm going to adopt."

Life is not always that easy. There isn't any way to prevent someone from experiencing pain, but learning about God's love is the best way to deal with life's ups and downs. God never promised that He would always protect us from pain and suffering, but He did say that He would walk with us through it and deliver us.

When you get into a tight place and
everything goes against you till it seems
as though you could not hold on a minute
longer, never give up, for that is just the
place and time that the tide will turn.

HARRIET BEECHER STOWE

BIG BROTHER

T ara looked at the big bully in front of her and stuck out her tongue. She knew she was taking life and limb in hand by being so reckless, but at this point, she really didn't care. She was tired of being pushed around, tired of being made fun of, and tired of handing over her lunch money to a boy who didn't appear to need another morsel of food for the next fifteen years.

Contend, Lord, with those who contend with me; fight against those who fight against me.

PSALM 35:1

Plus, she had a backup plan, a card she had been holding close to her chest—a card that would forever relieve her of intimidation from this bully. As it happened, today was the day to stand up and fight.

"You little . . ." The big boy took three menacing steps in Tara's direction, then stopped in his tracks. Looking over her left shoulder and then her right, the bully began to tremble and slowly backed up. Tara stood quietly as her three older brothers walked past her and continued to advance on the boy.

Her oldest brother, Peter, grabbed the boy's shirt and pulled him close. "This is your one warning—your only warning." He spoke slowly, dramatically. "Mess with our sister again, and we'll personally see to it that you never eat lunch again, or dinner, or breakfast . . . or anything. Understand?"

The boy nodded, refusing to look at Tara, then turned and ran.

God is our Protector. If we bring Him into the battles of daily life, there is no enemy that He cannot conquer with a simple word. He is better than a protective big brother. He is the ultimate Knight who fights the battles we cannot fight on our own.

Maybe no one is stealing your lunch money, but perhaps you're allowing something or someone to steal your joy, your peace, and your passion for life. Allow the King of Kings to step in and fight for you. He loves you and will never abandon you. He loves taking on the bad guys to bring lightness, peace, and confidence to your step. There is no bully alive that He cannot conquer.

Abraham did not know the way , but he knew the guide.

LEE ROBERSON

SWEET TOOTH

Eleven-year-old Gracie opened the refrigerator door, enjoying the cold draft of air after her walk home from the bus stop. She took a long swig of water from the pitcher, then headed straight for the cookie jar. Her sweet tooth demanded to be satisfied! Unfortunately, the cookie jar was empty. Before Sissy had left for college, it had always been full of Gracie's favorites: peanut butter.

She had watched her older sister make peanut-butter cookies hundreds of times. Why couldn't she do it herself? She didn't even need a cookbook. With a determined spirit, Gracie gathered all the ingredients for her first baking attempt — butter, vanilla, sugar, eggs, baking soda, peanut butter — and creamed the mixture together. She tasted the dough. It was almost as good as Sissy's. But something was missing. Flour!

Gracie opened the flour canister, but it was empty too. Maybe she could substitute something, she peered into every cabinet, stretching up on her tiptoes, until she spotted a brown paper bag with a dusting of flour on the outside. She scrambled up on the kitchen counter, retrieved the sack from the top shelf, and looked inside. Flour! It was all she needed. Gracie eagerly stirred in the flour to make a stiff dough and dropped the mixture by spoonfuls onto the cookie sheet. Then she used a fork to make the crisscrosses on top and popped the pan into the oven. She could hardly wait!

When the cookies were golden brown, she removed them from the oven and set them aside to cool. But she couldn't wait; her mouth was actually watering as she tasted her first bite.

"Yuck!" she exclaimed. It was salty! Gracie spit the cookie out in the sink just as her mother came in and discovered her daughter had used the coating mixture for frying chicken.

Sometimes a small substitution might not seem important, but the wrong ingredient can ruin the whole recipe. It's the same way in our walk with God. Little white lies might not seem that important, until they spoil the day.

A lie stands on one leg, truth on two.

BENJAMIN FRANKLIN

THE KEY INGREDIENT

"He's coming home, honey!" Caroline shouted to her husband.

Their son, Brad, had left home for college a few months earlier, leaving their home much too quite and empty. The phone hardly ever rang, and the doorbell remained silent. His absence took a toll on Caroline's emotions, causing her to retreat from the things that she'd always enjoyed.

> This is the day the Lord has made; let us rejoice and be glad in it.
>
> PSALM 118:24

Now he was coming to visit. Excitedly, she changed the sheets on his cold bed, remembering the many nights she knelt beside him as he said his bedtime prayers. For the last few months, she had wished so many times that she could kiss him goodnight before retiring for the evening. After she fluffed his pillow and straightened up his bedroom, she breezed into the kitchen to bake his favorite dessert—a buttermilk pound cake.

All the ingredients were on hand, and she almost had the recipe memorized. She measured them out carefully and made every effort to mix it as directed, but before all the flour was mixed in, the phone rang. After a brief conversation, she returned to the cake. She poured the batter into the baking pans and hurriedly placed them in the preheated oven.

About halfway through the baking time, she looked

into the mixing bowl. *Oh, no!* She had left out a large portion of the flour! A quick glance into the oven confirmed her fears; the cake was not rising. She was so disappointed. Despite her good intentions, she had left out most of an important ingredient. The cake might taste okay, but it would be flat and gooey.

Life is a lot like that cake. Some experiences may seem to be good and offer happiness, but without Christ, the most important element of life is missing. Do you have all the ingredients for a fulfilled life?

People can meet superficial needs. But only God can meet our deep needs.

FORRESTER BARRINGTON

THINK ON
THESE THINGS

Irene Harrell, author or coauthor of more than two dozen books, once wrote about an argument she had with one of her teenage sons. She recalled clenching her fists and gritting her teeth in anger. The teen had spared no expense in irritating his mother, and she was ready for a verbal fight. But the boy was saved by the bell—the telephone. By the time Irene had finished the call, her son was nowhere in sight.

Later that day as Irene went about her household chores, she complained to her younger son, James, about her older son's transgressions. After finishing a load of dishes, she found her young son deep in thought.

"I think I know what would help you with Tommy," James said. Not knowing what to do with her teenager, she listened carefully to her son's advice. "Just don't think about it," he said matter-of-factly.

While she swept the kitchen floor, this childlike suggestion rolled around in her mind. Then she turned her thoughts to God, concentrating on His grace and

Finally, brothers and sisters, whatever is true, whatever is noble, whatever is right, whatever is pure, whatever is lovely, whatever is admirable—if anything is excellent or praiseworthy—think about such things.

PHILIPPIANS 4:8

mercy.

Later, when her teenage son came home, she was able to treat him with this same mercy. Instead of an angry mother, Tommy found grace as Irene offered him an ice-cream float before he went to bed. She was surprised to find her son, who'd been braced for a scolding, responding in love. To her great surprise, the boy washed his glass and spoon that evening and mumbled, "Thanks, Mom," as he shuffled off to bed. The next morning, a change had come over her son. Irene found him lying in bed, smiling, and actually doing his homework.

Is there someone who needs your forgiveness? Today, think on these things—whatever is noble, right, pure, lovely, or admirable![30]

Mercy comes down from heaven to earth
so that man by practicing it may resemble
God.

GIAMBATTISTA GIRALDI

JOY IN THE MORNING

"**G**uess what I've got!" Grace shouted. Her two sons raced in to see what was in the box.

> Weeping may remain for a night, but rejoicing comes in the morning.
>
> PSALM 30:5

"It's a kitty," whispered four-year-old Donnie. A smile played around his mouth. Hesitantly, he reached inside and stroked the orange tabby's head. "What's his name?"

"He kind of reminds me of a ball of sunshine," his mother said. "Why don't we call him Sunny?" Recently divorced, Grace hoped the new kitten would help the boys get over their loneliness for their father.

"Let's feed the kitty," she said as she opened a can of cat food. The whirring of the can opener excited Sunny, and he climbed up her pants leg. Gently, she pulled the kitten from her, setting him in front of his food. Donnie and his brother watched the kitten eat every mouthful.

But as evening shadows crossed the room, Grace felt depression stalking her again. How would she ever raise her sons without any help? The divorce had not been easy, and the emotional battering had taken its toll. Later that night, she lay in bed, still battling the sadness.

The next morning, Donnie crawled into bed with her and the kitten. With sunlight streaming through slatted blinds, they cuddled and watched Sunny swat at dust balls. It was easy to smile at the kitten's antics, but she wondered if she would ever be happy again.

Donnie picked up the kitten and put him on his lap. Gently, the boy patted his head, then rubbed the kitten behind his ears. Soon the cat began to purr—loudly. Donnie leaned down and listened, his eyes widening in surprise. "Mom, my kitty's swallowed a motorcycle!" he said. Grace burst into laughter, rejoicing that God had given her such wonderful children.

Sometimes, we all sink into a well of discouragement. When that happens, thank God for the small things of life, even when you're walking in the valley of shadows. Let Him turn your weeping into joy.

To get the full value of a joy, you must
have somebody to divide it with.

MARK TWAIN

THE TATTERED BIBLE

Sarah's worn and tattered cookbook sat on a desk in the corner of the kitchen. Some of its pages were stuck together with drops of cake batter or cookie dough. Practically every page was stained, but it was obvious which recipes were her favorites. Those pages were barely readable. Between the leaves of the book were recipes from newspapers and store packages that she had carefully cut out over the years.

> Let the word of Christ dwell in you richly as you teach and admonish one another with all wisdom.
>
> COLOSSIANS 3:16

Sarah couldn't get along in the kitchen without her trusted cookbook. Not only did it provide a list of ingredients needed and instructions for preparing her favorite dishes, it also provided many useful facts to enable her to run her kitchen efficiently.

"Learning to read a recipe correctly is the most important part of cooking," she told her daughter many times.

Sitting close beside that trusted cookbook was her Bible. Like the cookbook, its pages were worn. It held clippings of memorable events that had taken place in her life and the lives of her family members over the years. Ink spots dotted the pages of her favorite Scripture passages. After many years of use, certain verses were difficult to read.

"Learning to understand the Bible and using it as a guideline for life is the most important part of living," she told her daughter. "This is God's instruction book designed especially for us. Everything that you will ever need to know about life is written on these pages."

By her example, Sarah taught her daughter that a used Bible is the most valuable tool for living. She sought God's guidance through His Word on a regular basis. Not only had it provided her with security and hope, it also helped her to live a life pleasing to Him.

That tattered Bible explained a lot about Sarah's life. All the ingredients and instructions were there; she only needed to follow them in order to find the strength, wisdom, and courage that characterized her life.

The bible is the cornerstone of liberty.

THOMAS JEFFERSON

COMING HOME

Amanda trudged through the snow on the Connecticut hillside. It had been a great afternoon of sledding, playing, and throwing snowballs. She had thrown the perfect snowball at her teenage son, Cody. He'd grinned, looked at her through snow-covered eyelashes, and shouted, "Nice shot, Mom! But look out! I'll get you back!" Amanda had attempted to run but didn't get far before her mischievous son had helped her land face-first in the soft snow.

Now they made their way back on the seemingly endless snow-covered path. By the time Amanda opened the front door to their home, she could barely feel her nose, ears, or fingertips. "We're back!" she called to her mother, who was busy making hot chocolate in the kitchen.

Amanda and the children peeled off their frozen layers and settled into the warmth of the living room couches. Grandmother bustled in with cups of steaming hot cocoa, and the smell from the kitchen indicated warm cookies were on the way. Amanda curled her fingers around the heated cup and smiled at the rosy cheeks of her offspring. There was nothing like it! Nothing eclipsed

However, as it is written: "What no eye has seen, what no ear has heard, and what no human mind has conceived"—the things God has prepared for those who love him . . .

1 CORINTHIANS 2:9

the feelings of home, of warmth, of coming in from the cold to the waiting hot chocolate.

God is preparing us. He watches from the window as we make our way across the cold and barren land-scape. The minute we walk through the door of Heaven, we will be overwhelmed with the love of a gracious, waiting Father. It will be a celebration of peace, of coming home — the feelings of pleasure and joy more intense than we can even imagine. No matter where you are today, no matter what pain or what joy you are experiencing, it is nothing compared to the pleasure you will know in the light of God's presence.

The knowledge that we are never alone
calms the troubled sea of our lives and
speaks peace to our souls.

A. W. TOZER

FUTURE FATHER

June surveyed the crowd before her. The noise seemed too much, almost overwhelming as everyone tried to speak at once. It was Sunday dinner, and all the family was gathered around the large table. Steaming platters of food were being handed from person to person as plates were piled higher and higher with delectable treats.

> "Whoever welcomes a little child like this in my name welcomes me."
>
> MATTHEW 18:5

Down near the end of the table sat Daniel, a friend of June's youngest child, Nate. Daniel was only eight years old and looked flustered and nervous as people passed food around and over him. June watched as one of the other children noticed and attended to him, asking, "Would you like some of these potatoes, Daniel?"

The small boy nodded and smiled a simple grin of appreciation. The others seemed to take notice of him then and began asking him questions about school and friends. June knew that Daniel had a difficult home life. She was proud of her children as they focused on his hopes and dreams and seemed genuinely interested. "What do you want to be when you grow up?" asked one of the children.

Daniel hesitated, looked around at the family, then said, "I want to be a Dad. With lots of kids, like this family."

The room got quiet as everyone mulled over what he had said. Finally Bob, the oldest, smiled broadly and patted him on the back. "Sounds great, Daniel! You'll make a great father!" he said, winking, "as long as you have a better group than this one to work with!"

The room exploded as all the kids laughed and began shouting over each other, yelling their defense. June watched Daniel in the rising commotion. He was sitting quietly with a smile on his face. Finally he grabbed his fork and seemed to nod to himself as he ate his first big bite. He seemed . . . triumphant.

Is there a little one you can love on today — someone in your home, your church, or your neighborhood? Just a few small words of encouragement, a pair of listening ears, or an afternoon in the midst of your family can make a difference in the life of a child.

There is a grace of kind listening, as well
as a grace of kind speaking.

FREDERICK WILLIAM FABER

LEAVE IT TO ME

Many people find it easier to commit their future into the Lord's hands than to commit the problems and concerns of the day. We recognize our helplessness in regard to the future, but we often feel as if the present is in our own hands.

A Christian by the name of Mary Ellen once had a great burden in her life. She was so distraught she could not sleep or eat. She was jeopardizing her physical and emotional health and was on the verge of a nervous breakdown. She recognized, however, that there wasn't anything *she* could do to change her circumstances.

> Cast your burden on the Lord [releasing the weight of it] and he will sustain you.
>
> PSALM 55:22 AMP

Then Mary Ellen read a story in a magazine about another woman, Connie, who also had major difficulties in her life. In the account, a friend asked Connie how she was able to bear up under the load of such troubles. She replied, "I take my problems to the Lord."

Connie's friend replied, "Of course, that is what we should do."

Then Connie added, "But we must not only *take* our problems there. We must *leave* our problems with the Lord."[31]

Not only are we to leave our problems with the Lord, but we are to hold nothing back.

There is a humorous story about an elderly man who vowed he would never ride in an airplane. However, one day an emergency arose, and it was necessary for him to get to a distant city in a hurry. The fastest way to get there was by air, of course, so he purchased a ticket and made his first trip in an airplane.

Knowing his reluctance to fly, when his relatives met him at the airport, they asked him how he enjoyed the flight. He responded, "Oh, it was all right, I guess. But I'll tell you one thing. I never let my *full weight* down on the seat."[32]

The Lord wants you to cast your burdens on Him—and leave them there! He desires for you to give Him the full weight of your problems as well. Then you can go on with life in full confidence He will take care of those things you have entrusted to Him.

We ought never to bear the burden of sin or doubt, but there are burdens placed on us by God, which he does not intend to lift off. He wants us to roll them back on him.

OSWALD CHAMBERS

QUALITY TIME

Busy — so busy! The sun has long since set, and there is still so much to do. Work, family, church, and much more seem to demand hours God never put in the day. Still, we Christians think all these accomplishments will please our Heavenly Father. After all, faith without works is dead, right?

When we finally fall into bed at night, can we say we've actually spent any time with the Father we're trying so hard to please?

In his book *Unto the Hills*, Billy Graham tells a story about a little girl and her father who were great friends and enjoyed spending time together. They went for walks and shared a passion for watching birds, enjoying the changing seasons, and meeting people who crossed their path.

One day, the father noticed a change in his daughter. If he went for a walk, she excused herself from going. Knowing she was growing up, he rationalized that she must be expected to lose interest in her Daddy as she made other friends. Nevertheless, her absence grieved him deeply.

Because of his daughter's absences, he was not in a particularly happy mood on his birthday. Then she presented him with a pair of exquisitely worked slippers, which she had hand made for him while he was out of the house walking.

At last he understood and said, "My darling, I like these slippers very much, but next time buy the slippers and let me have you all the days. I would rather have my child than anything she can make for me."[33]

Is it possible our Heavenly Father sometimes feels lonely for the company of His children? Are we so busy doing good deeds that we forget—or are too weary—to spend some quiet time with Him as our day draws to a close?

Take a walk with your Heavenly Father as the sun sets. Spend some quality time, talking to Him about anything and everything. You will be blessed, and so will He!

Time is the deposit each one has in the bank of God, and no one knows the balance.

RALPH WASHINGTON SOCKMAN

COME HOME

O nce there was a widow who lived in a miser-
able attic with her son. Years before, the
woman had married against her parents'
wishes and had gone to live in a
foreign land with her husband.
Her husband had proved irrespon-
sible and unfaithful, and after a
few years he died without having
made any provision for her and
their child. It was with the utmost
difficulty that she managed to
scrape together the bare necessities of life.

> "'This son
> of mine
> was dead
> and is alive
> again; he
> was lost
> and is
> found.'"
>
> LUKE 15:24

The happiest times in the child's life were when the
mother took him in her arms and told him about her
father's house in the old country. She told him of the
grassy lawn, the noble trees, the wild flowers, the lovely
paintings, and the delicious meals. The child had never
seen his grandfather's home, but to him it was the most
beautiful place in all the world. He longed for the time
when he would go to live there.

One day the postman knocked at the attic door. The
mother recognized the handwriting on the envelope, and
with trembling fingers she broke the seal. There was a
check and a slip of paper with just two words: "Come
home."[34]

Like this father — and the father of the Prodigal Son —
our Heavenly Father opens His arms to receive us back

into a place of spiritual comfort and restoration at the end of a weary day.

God does not ask us to stand and take our punishment for the day's failures. He simply welcomes us into His healing presence as children redeemed by the blood of His Son. There, He assures us that He understands our hurts and shortcomings and, miracle of all miracles, loves us anyway.

The Father is calling you to come home. Why not finish your day in the comfort and provision of His presence?

Nor can we fall below the arms of God,

how lowsoever it be we fall.

WILLIAM PENN

EVERYDAY NEEDS

"Oh, no! We're going to have to run for the ferry again!" Elaine cried. "And, unless we find a parking place in the next minute or two, we're never going to make it!"

As Elaine and her daughter, Cathy, struggled through the downtown Seattle traffic, she thought back to when they had moved to Bainbridge Island four years earlier. They had thought it to be a perfect, idyllic place. Her daughter was in high school, and Elaine could work part time at home.

Now college bills had made full-time work a necessity for Elaine. She, her husband, and Cathy were obliged to make the daily commute to Seattle via the ferry. With a car parked on both sides of the water, praying for parking spaces had become a daily event.

"I told you we needed to get away from your office sooner," Cathy chided. "You just can't count on finding a parking place within walking distance of the ferry when the waterfront is full of summer tourists and conventioneers!"

> This is the confidence we have in approaching God: that if we ask anything according to his will, he hears us. And if we know that he hears us—whatever we ask—we know that we have what we asked of him.
>
> 1 JOHN 5:14-15

"God knew about that last-minute customer I had, and He knows we have to make this ferry in order to get home in time to fix dinner and make it to the church meeting," Elaine assured her. Then she prayed aloud, "Lord, we'll circle this block one more time. Please have someone back out, or we're not going to make it."

"Mom, there it is!" Cathy shouted, as they rounded the last corner. "Those people just got in their car. I have to admit—sometimes you have a lot more faith than I do. Who'd think God would be interested in whether or not we find a parking place?"

"But that's the exciting part of it," Elaine explained. "God is interested in every part of our lives—even schedules and parking places. Now, let's run for it!"[35]

The Lord knows all the circumstances of your day—and your tomorrow. Trust Him to be the "Lord of the details."

You may trust the Lord too little, but you
can never trust him too much.

UNKNOWN

FRAGMENTS

Margaret Brownley tells of her son's first letters from camp:

> *When my oldest son went away to summer camp for the first time, I was a nervous wreck. Although he was nine years old, he hadn't as much as spent a night away from home, let alone an entire week. I packed his suitcase with special care, making sure he had enough socks and underwear to see him through the week. I also packed stationery and stamps so he could write home.*
>
> *I received the first letter from him three days after he left for camp. I quickly tore open the envelope and stared at the childish scrawl, which read: Camp is fun, but the food is yucky! The next letter offered little more: Jerry wet the bed. "Who's Jerry?" I wondered. The third and final letter had this interesting piece of news: The nurse said it's not broken.*
>
> *Fragments. Bits of information that barely skim the surface. A preview of coming attractions that never materialize. It made me think of my own sparse messages to God. "Dear Lord," I plead when a son is late coming home, "keep him safe." Or, "Give me strength," I pray when faced with a difficult neighbor or the challenge of*

> One day Jesus was praying in a certain place. When he finished, one of his disciples said to him, "Lord, teach us to pray."
>
> LUKE 11:1

a checkbook run amuck. "Let me have wisdom," is another favorite prayer of mine, usually murmured in haste while waiting my turn at a parent/teacher conference or dealing with a difficult employee. "Thank-you, God," I say before each meal or when my brood is tucked in safely for the night.

Fragments. Bits and pieces. Are my messages to God as unsatisfactory to Him as my son's letters were to me? With a guilty start, I realized that it had been a long time since I'd had a meaningful chat with the Lord.

When my son came home, he told me all about his adventures. It was good to have him home and safe. "Thank-you, God," I murmured, and then caught myself. It was time I sent God more than just a hasty note from "camp."[36]

Cultivate the thankful spirit! It will be to
you a perpetual feast.

JOHN R. MACDUFF

ALL THE DETAILS

Andrea was in no mood for her six-year-old son's Saturday morning antics. While Steven argued with his friends over video games, Andrea stewed over her own mounting pile of pressures. Just-bought groceries for tomorrow's dinner guests sprawled across every bit of counter space. Buried under them was a Sunday school lesson to be prepared. A week's worth of laundry spilled out of the laundry room into the kitchen, and an upsetting letter from a faraway friend in need lay teetering on the edge of the sink.

In the midst of this turmoil, Steven's Sunday-school teacher called. "Is Steven going to the carnival with us this afternoon?"

"He didn't mention anything about it."

"Well, we'll be leaving about noon. If he didn't bring home his permission slip, just write the usual information on a slip of paper and send it along with him." As soon as Andrea reminded Steven about the trip, his mood changed, and he was his "better self" for the next couple of hours.

Andrea was just pulling a cake from the oven when she heard the doorbell ring, followed by an awful commotion. Rushing to the living room, she found two little girls waving pink slips of paper at her crying son. "What's the matter?" she asked as she gently put her arms around him.

"I can't go!" he wailed. "I don't have one of those pink papers!"

"Oh, yes you do. Only yours happens to be white," she said as she dried his tears, stuffed the paper in his pocket, and sent him out the door.

Back in the kitchen Andrea wondered, "Why didn't he just ask me about the paper? Hasn't he been my child long enough to know I'd have a solution?"

Suddenly a tiny smile crept across her face as she surveyed the chaos around her—and she could almost hear her Heavenly Father say, "Haven't you been My child long enough to know that I have it taken care of?[37]

Trust God where you cannot trace him.
Do not try to penetrate the cloud he
brings over to you; rather look to the bow
that is on it. The mystery is God's; the
promise is yours.

JOHN R. MACDUFF

HEAVEN'S SPOT REMOVER

"Let it snow; let it snow; let it snow." That's the cry of school-aged children everywhere when winter weather finally arrives.

First, there's catching those early snowflakes on your tongue. After a few more flakes hit the ground, you snowballs and have some terrific battles. Several inches later, it's time to build the snowmen and snow forts. And when the blanket of snow reaches a hefty thickness, the best thing to do is make snow angels.

> It is of the Lord's mercies that we are not consumed, because his compassions fail not. They are new every morning: great is thy faithfulness
>
> LAMENTATIONS 3:22-23 KJV

Remember snow angels? You find a good patch of untouched snow, stand with your arms stretched out to the side, and fall backwards onto what feels like a cold, wet cloud. Stay on your back for a few moments and stare at the sky. When the cold starts getting to you, flap your arms and legs as if you're doing jumping jacks. Then, carefully get up and look at your handiwork.

Between the snowballs and snowmen, the forts and the angels, it isn't long before every square inch of clean snow has been used up. Patches of dead grass show through where someone dug down deep to roll a snowman's head. The once-pristine landscape is now trampled and rutted.

But something magical happens overnight. While you are sleeping, the snow falls again. You look out your window in the morning to find another clean white blanket covering all of the previous day's blemishes. All that was ugly is once again beautiful.

Don't despair when what began as a beautiful day turns into something ugly. Even though our own efforts to "fix it up" or "clean it up" might be futile, it can still be redeemed. The God who turned the humiliation and shame of His Son's death on the cross into the gift of salvation for all who believe in Him, can take the tattered rags of our daily lives and make them like new again— every morning.

When God's goodness cannot be seen, his mercy can be experienced.

ROBERT HAROLD SCHULLER

A SABBATH

What is it that gives you that warm fuzzy feeling inside? Certain smells, like the aroma of homemade bread right out of the oven or hot apple cider, make you feel everything will be all right. Certain sounds—a crackling fire in the fireplace that chases away the damp chill on a rainy night; the whistling of a teakettle, ready to brew a pot of your favorite tea; the beauty of Beethoven's "Moonlight Sonata" —all make you feel that life is good.

> Be glad and rejoice for ever in that which I create.
>
> ISAIAH 65:18 RSV

To Oscar Hammerstein, that warm, fuzzy, everything-is-going-to-be-okay feeling came from "whiskers on kittens and warm, woolen mittens." What are some of your favorite things? When was the last time you gave yourself permission to be "nonproductive" and enjoy some of life's simple pleasures—like the beauty of a sunset?

Logan Pearsall Smith wrote, "If you are losing your leisure, look out! You may be losing your soul." When we don't take time for leisure or relaxation, when we give our discretionary time away to busyness and relentless activity, we are living in a way that says, "everything depends upon me and my efforts."

Consequently, God prescribed a day of rest, the Sabbath, to enjoy His creation and to give us time to reflect and remember all He has done for us and all He is. The

Sabbath is time to remember God is God—and we're not!

The Sabbath doesn't have to be Sunday. You can take a Sabbath rest anytime you relax and turn your focus to God and His creation. Sometimes you have nothing better to do than relax. You may have something *else* to do, but you don't have anything *better* to do.

Relax and just enjoy God's creation. After all, He *created* it for you to enjoy.

Jesus knows we must come apart and rest awhile, or else we may just plain come apart.

VANCE HAVNER

SHALOM

A word that appears throughout the Old Testament is shalom. It is often translated "peace," but shalom means far more than peace in the aftermath of war or peace between enemies. Shalom embodies an inner peace which brings wholeness, unity, and balance to an individual's life. It describes a harmonious, nurturing environment which has God at its center.

> "Peace I leave with you, my peace I give unto you."
>
> JOHN 14:27 KJV

In creation, God brought order and harmony out of chaos. He created shalom. It was people's sin that destroyed shalom, but it has always been God's plan that it be restored—first to the human heart and then, flowing from that, to heart-to-heart relationships.

In the book of Revelation, we have the glorious hope that the Prince of Peace will rule over a new heaven and earth that are described as perfect. According to Isaiah, justice, righteousness, and peace will characterize His unending kingdom. The Prince of Shalom will restore God's original shalom!

God has given us many promises for peace in His word. Meditate on His promises of shalom, and as you do, they will flood your heart and mind with peace, cleansing you from the stress of the day.

• Since we have been justified through faith, we have peace with God through our Lord Jesus Christ (Romans 5:1).

• Great peace have they who love your law, and nothing can make them stumble (Psalm 119:165).

• When a man's ways are pleasing to the Lord, he makes even his enemies live at peace with him (Proverbs 16:7).

• May the God of hope fill you with all joy and peace as you trust in him, so that you may overflow with hope (Romans 15:13).

• The peace of God, which transcends all understanding, will guard your hearts and your minds in Christ Jesus (Philippians 4:7).

You can have peace with God, peace in your walk, and peace with your enemies. Shalom!

First keep the peace within yourself, then
you can also bring peace to others.

THOMAS À KEMPIS

FIVE MINUTES

In peace I will both lie down and sleep; for thou alone, O Lord, makes me dwell in safety.

PSALM 4:8 RSV

I f you wake up as weary as you were when you went to bed the night before, try to recall what you were thinking about the last five minutes before you went to sleep. What you think about in that five minutes impacts how well you sleep, which determines what kind of day tomorrow will be.

When you sleep, your conscious mind is at rest, but your subconscious mind remains active. Psychologists call the subconscious the "assistant manager of life." When the conscious mind is "off duty," the subconscious mind takes over. The subconscious carries out the orders that are given to it, even though you are not aware of it.

For example, if the last minutes before going to sleep are spent in worry, the subconscious records and categorizes that as fear and acts as if the fear is reality. Thus muscles remain tense, nerves are on edge, and the body's organs are upset, which means the body is not really at rest.

However, if those last five minutes are spent contemplating some great idea, an inspiring verse, or a calm and reassuring thought, it will signal to the nervous system, "All is well," and put the entire body in a relaxed, peaceful state. This helps you to wake up refreshed, strengthened, and confident.

Many of the days that begin badly started out that way because of the night before, during those critical last five minutes of conscious thought. You can input positive, healthy thoughts into your conscious mind and pave the way for quiet, restful sleep by simply meditating on God's Word as you drop off to sleep. For example, Psalms 91:1-2 NKJV: "HE who dwells in the secret place of the Most High Shall abide under the shadow of the Almighty. I will say of the Lord, '*He is* my refuge and my fortress; My God, in Him I will trust.'"

Sweet dreams!

Our pursuit of God is successful just
because he is forever seeking to manifest
himself to us.

A. W. TOZER

SERENITY

Many people are familiar with the "Serenity" prayer, although most probably think of it as a prayer to be said in the morning hours or during a time of crisis. Consider again the words of this prayer: "God, grant me the Serenity to accept the things I cannot change, Courage to change the things I can, and Wisdom to know the difference."

Can there be any better prayer to say at the day's end? Those things which are irreversible or fixed in God's order, we need to relinquish to Him. True peace of mind comes when we trust that God knows more about any situation than we could possibly know. He can turn any situation from bad to good in His timing and according to His methods.

Those things we can change, we must have the courage to change. Furthermore, we must accept the fact that in most cases we cannot change things until morning comes! We can rest in the interim, knowing the Lord will help us when the time comes for action.

The real heart of the Serenity prayer is revealed in its conclusion, that we might know the difference between

Vindicate me, O Lord, for I have walked in my integrity; I have [relied on and] trusted [confidently] in the Lord without wavering and I shall not slip.

PSALM 26:1 AMP

what we need to accept and what we need to change. That takes wisdom. James tells us, "If any of you is deficient in wisdom, let him ask of the giving God [Who gives] to everyone liberally *and* ungrudgingly, without reproaching *or* faultfinding, and it will be given him. Only it must be in faith that he asks with no wavering (no hesitating, no doubting)" (James 1:5-6 AMP).

At day's end, we must recognize the Lord's wisdom may not be given to us before we sleep, but perhaps as we sleep, so that when we awaken, we have the answer we need. Many people have reported this to be true. They went to bed having a problem, turned it over to God in prayer, and awoke with a solution that seemed "plain as day" in the morning light.

Ask the Lord to give you true serenity tonight!

Invariable mark of wisdom is to see the
miraculous in the common.

JAMES RUSSELL LOWELL

WHAT DO YOU WANT?

Children are quick to respond to their environment. Babies immediately cry when they are hungry, thirsty, tired, sick, or wet. Toddlers are not at all bashful in communicating what they do and do not want. However, as we grow older, maturity teaches us to use discernment in making our desires known and to give way to the needs of others in many situations.

The Lord nevertheless tells us we are wise to always come to Him as little children—telling Him precisely what we need and want. While looking directly at a man whom He knew was blind, Jesus asked him, "What do you want Me to do for you?" Without hesitation he replied, "Master, let me receive my sight" (Mark 10:51 AMP).

Jesus could see he was blind, yet He asked him to make a request. In like manner, God knows what you need "before you ask Him" (Matthew 6:8 AMP). Yet He says in His Word, "by prayer and petition (definite requests) . . . continue to make your wants known to God" (Philippians 4:6 AMP).

Why pray for what seems to be obvious? Because in

"I thank You and praise You, O God of my fathers, For You have given me wisdom and power; Even now You have made known to me what we requested of You . . ."

DANIEL 2:23 AMP

stating precisely what we want, our needs and desires become obvious to us.

If we stop to listen to our own petitions, we come face to face with our priorities, our hurts, and our excesses. We see ourselves more clearly and thus have an opportunity for repentance. We see the core of an issue — something we may have skirted or refused to handle. At other times, we know precisely where we need to take action or say to someone, "Enough is enough."

State your requests boldly before the Lord tonight. He'll hear you. He'll respond to you. And just as important, you'll hear yourself and respond in a new way to Him.

———————————————

Our prayers must mean something to us
if they are to mean anything to God.

MALTBIE D. BABCOCK

SHINING THROUGH

A little girl was among a group of people being given a guided tour through a great cathedral. As the guide explained the various parts of the structure—the altar, the choir, the screen, and the nave—the little girl's attention was intently focused on a stained glass window.

> Let your light so shine before men, that they may see your good works and glorify your Father in heaven.
>
> MATTHEW 5:16
> NKJV

For a long time she silently pondered the window. Looking up at the various figures, her face was bathed in a rainbow of color as the afternoon sun poured into the transept of the huge cathedral.

As the group was about to move on, she gathered enough courage to ask the tour conductor a question. "Who are those people in that pretty window?"

"Those are the saints," the guide replied.

That night, as the little girl was preparing for bed, she told her mother proudly: "I know who the saints are."

"Oh?" replied the mother. "And just who are the saints?"

Without a moment's hesitation the little girl replied: "They are the people who let the light shine through!"[38]

As you look back over your day, did you let God's light shine through? Sometimes we pass these opportunities by, saying, "It will just take too much out of me."

But the Bible lets us know that everything we give will come back to us—multiplied. (See Luke 6:38.)

We see this principle in nature. A microscopic speck of radium can send out a stream of sparks which give off light and heat, yet in emitting the light and heat, it does not deplete itself of its own energy.

As Christians we are called to share the light of Jesus in a world of darkness. Like rays of light that break through gloom and darkness, we can bring hope and encouragement.

Remember, the light of your life gives those around you a glimpse of Jesus, the Source of eternal and constant light. As you let your light shine, it will grow brighter!

Should first my lamp spread light and
purest rays bestow,
the oil must then from you, my dearest
Jesus, flow.

ANGELUS SILEIUS

LIKE A CHILD

> "I assure you and most solemnly say to you, whoever does not receive and welcome the kingdom of God like a child will not enter it at all."
>
> MARK 10:15 AMP

Many parents have stood in awe by the beds of their sleeping children, amazed at the miracle of their lives, captured by their sweet expressions of innocence, and bewildered by their ability to sleep peacefully regardless of the turmoil that may be around them.

Those same parents have also felt great frustration earlier in the day when their children were willful or disobedient, and they marveled at their children's ingenuity, energy, curiosity, or humor. Children seem to embody all of life's extremes.

What did Jesus mean when He said we must receive and welcome the kingdom of God as a little child? Surely He meant we must accept and embrace God's will for our lives with a sense that "this is what is, and isn't it grand"—welcoming the Lord's will; not with debate, question, worry, or fear; but with a sense of delight, expectation, and eagerness.

As a child opens a present, he or she has no doubt that the pretty paper and ribbon hide a happy surprise.

In the same way, we must anticipate that the kingdom of God is a joyful and wonderful gift to us, one in which we can delight thoroughly.

Andrew Gillies has written a lovely poem to describe the childlikeness the Lord desires to see in us.

Last night my little boy confessed to me
Some childish wrong;
And kneeling at my knee,
He prayed with tears –
"Dear God, make me a man like Daddy –
Wise and strong; I know you can!"
Then while he slept I knelt beside his bed,
Confessed my sins,
And prayed with low-bowed head –
"O God, make me a child like my child here –
Pure, guileless,
Trusting Thee with faith sincere."[39]

Be content to be a child, and let the father
proportion out daily to thee what light,
what power, what exercise, what straits,
what fears, what troubles he sees fit for
thee.

ISAAC PENINGTON

THINK ON THESE THINGS

In a recent study, twenty-two women experiencing "high-anxiety" were hooked up to heart monitors and told to spend ten minutes watching the beat of their pulses on special wristwatches. After twelve weeks of this, all of the women had definite improvement in their anxiety levels.

> His delight is in the law of the Lord, and on his law he meditates day and night.
>
> PSALM 1:2

An additional thirty-three women were tested at the same time. Their anxiety-reducing exercise was reading magazines. Reading proved less effective than simply watching a pulse beat. What is it about taking ten minutes to watch your heartbeat that makes one less anxious?

One of the doctors involved in the study said that when you sit and focus on these steady rhythms, you are forced to remain in the moment. Dedicating yourself to this task for ten minutes takes your mind off both the past and the future — the two hobgoblins of modern life.

There are 960 working minutes in a day (if you allow eight hours for sleep). This doctor points out that all of us can find ten minutes for this simple form of "meditation" — especially when the payoff is less stress.[40]

In the Bible, God commanded Joshua to engage in a different kind of exercise: "Do not let this Book of the Law depart from your mouth; meditate on it day and night" (Joshua 1:8).

When Joshua meditated on God's Word, he was focusing on something that would help him live a righteous life at that moment. Foremost in his mind was the question, "What does God want me to do right now? How can I keep my finger on God's pulse?"

As you lie in bed tonight, place your hand over your heart and feel the pulse of your physical life for a few minutes. Then turn your attention to the pulse of your spiritual life, Jesus Christ, who lives in your heart.

Ask Jesus what He would like you to be thinking about as you fall asleep.

Who brought me hither will bring me
hence; no other guide I seek.

JOHN MILTON

HOME FIRES

Ernestine Schuman-Heink is not the first to ask, "What is a home?" But her answer is one of the most beautiful ever penned:

A roof to keep out the rain. Four walls to keep out the wind. Floors to keep out the cold. Yes, but home is more than that. It is the laugh of a baby, the song of a mother, the strength of a father. Warmth of loving hearts, light from happy eyes, kindness, loyalty, comradeship. Home is first school and first church for young ones, where they learn what is right, what is good and what is kind. Where they go for comfort when they are hurt or sick. Where fathers and mothers are respected and loved. Where children are wanted. Where the simplest food is good enough for kings because it is earned. Where money is not so important as lovingkindness. Where even the teakettle sings from happiness. That is home. God bless it.[41]

> Teach the young women to be sober, to love their husbands, to love their children.
>
> TITUS 2:4 KJV

God asks us to call Him "Father," and family life is at the heart of the Gospel. Through Jesus Christ, God the Father has forged a way to adopt many children. As a result, the Scriptures have much to say about what a happy home should be like. Good family life is never an accident, but an achievement by those who share it.

When our Heavenly Father is the Center of our homes,

our homes will be a reflection of Him. But sometimes this is easier said than done. That's why He gave us sixty-six books of the Bible to help us! We must learn His way of thinking and doing things. Then we must teach our children what He teaches us.

Keeping the home fires burning is letting God's Word and presence guide your way and keeping the love of God ablaze in the hearts of your family.

The home is a lighthouse which has the
lamp of God on the table and the light of
Christ in the window to give guidance to
those who wander in darkness.

HENRY RISCHE

THE DINNER TABLE

I n our modern society, with frantic schedules, fast-food restaurants, and microwave ovens, family members frequently "catch a meal" whenever and wherever they can, eating it "on the run."

> He took bread, gave thanks and broke it, and gave it to them.
>
> LUKE 22:19
> NKJV

Nevertheless, when we reflect upon the good times we have shared with family members, our memories often settle upon family meals — not necessarily holiday feasts, but daily family dinner conversations. When we sit at a table with one another, we not only share food, but also our lives.

Elton Trueblood has written eloquently about family dinnertime. Perhaps it's time we reinstitute this practice in our lives! She writes:

The table is really the family altar! Here those of all ages come together and help to sustain both their physical and their spiritual existence. If a sacrament is "an actual conveyance of spiritual meaning and power by a material process," then a family meal can be a sacrament. It entwines the material and the spiritual in a remarkable way. The food, in and of itself, is purely physical, but it represents human service in its use. Here, at one common table, is the father who has earned, the mother who has prepared or planned, and the children who share, according to need, whatever their antecedent participa-

tion may have been.

When we realize how deeply a meal together can be a spiritual and regenerating experience, we can understand something of why our Lord, when he broke bread with his little company toward the end of their earthly fellowship, told them, as often as they did it, to remember him.

We, too, seek to be members of his sacred fellowship, and irrespective of what we do about the Eucharist, there is no reason why each family meal should not take on something of the character of a time of memory and hope.[42]

When was the last time your family gathered together for a meal?

The family circle is the supreme
conductor of christianity.

HENRY DRUMMOND

STARGAZING

Then He brought him outside and said, "Look now toward heaven, and count the stars if you are able to number them." And He said to him, "So shall your descendants be."

GENESIS 15:5
NKJV

While visiting relatives in a rural area, a father decided to take his young daughter for an evening walk along a country road. The family lived in a large city, where walking at night was not the custom or considered safe. The father could hardly wait to see how his daughter would respond to a star-filled sky.

At first, his daughter was playful, exploring the flowers and insects along the edge of the dirt lane. As dusk turned into dark, however, she became a little fearful and clung to his hand tightly. She seemed grateful for the flashlight he had brought along. Suddenly, she looked toward the sky and exclaimed with surprise, "Daddy, somebody drew dots all over the sky!"

Her father smiled. His young daughter had never seen a night sky away from the city lights. He was glad the moon had not yet risen so the stars appeared even closer and more distinct. "Daddy," she continued in her enthusiasm, "if we connect them all, will they make a picture?"

The night sky had taken on the quality of a dot-to-dot puzzle for his child! *What an interesting notion*, the father thought. "No," he replied to his daughter, "the dots are there for another purpose. Each one is a hope God has for your life. God loves you so much He has lots of hopes that your life will be filled with good things. In fact, there are more hopes than you or I can ever count!"

"I knew it!" the little girl said. "The dots do make a picture." And then she added more thoughtfully, "I always wondered what hope looked like."

When God showed Abraham the stars and asked him to count them, He was giving him hope that the promise He had made to him, that he would have a son, was coming.

Whenever the sky is clear at night, do some stargazing! The stars are a picture of God's hope—for you, for your family, for the world. Stargazing is one of the best ways to get your earthy life back into perspective and realize that in God's infinite universe, He has a specific plan for you, just as He did for Abraham.

Eternity is the divine treasure house, and
hope is the window, by which mortals are
permitted to see, as through a glass
darkly, the things which God is preparing.

WILLIAM MOUNTFORD

FAMILY DEVOTIONS

Bedtime prayers are often limited to reciting a poem or saying a little memorized prayer. However, bedtime prayers can become family devotions if the entire family gathers at the bedside of the child who retires first.

Each member of the family says a heartfelt prayer that is spontaneous and unrehearsed. A verse or two of Scripture might be read prior to prayer. The point of such a devotional time is not that children are obedient to say a prayer before sleep, but that the children's hearts are knit to the heart of God and to the hearts of other family members.

Spontaneous, unrehearsed prayers invite children to share their hearts with the Lord. Having family members pray allows the children to catch a glimpse of others' souls and learn from their example how to relate to God, give praise, and make their requests known to a loving Heavenly Father.

Albert Schweitzer once commented on the need for parents to provide an example in devotion:

But you, when you pray, go into your room, and when you have shut your door, pray to your Father who is in the secret place; and your Father who sees in secret will reward you openly.

MATTHEW 6:6 NKJV

From the services in which I joined as a child I have taken with me into life a feeling for what is solemn, and a need for quiet self-recollection, without which I cannot realize the meaning of my life. I cannot, therefore, support the opinion of those who would not let children take part in grown-up people's services till they to some extent understand them. The important thing is not that they shall understand but that they shall feel something of what is serious and solemn. The fact that a child sees his elders full of devotion, and has to feel something of devotion himself, that is what gives the service its meaning for him.[43]

End your evening with family devotions. Even if you don't have children, it's an opportunity to spend time with your Heavenly Father and sort out the chaos of the day. He'll help you put everything into perspective so you can sleep peacefully.

When I am with God my fear is gone; in
the great quiet of god my troubles are as
the pebbles on the road, my joys are like
the everlasting hills.

WALTER RAUSCHENBUSCH

GOD IS AWAKE

Anna was alone in her new home for the first time. Jake's new job meant they would some-day be able to buy a home of their own in a safer part of town. But for now, they could only afford a rental house in a section where drug deals and street-walkers were a daily sight.

> He will not let your foot slip—he who watches over you will not slumber; indeed, he who watches over Israel will neither slumber nor sleep.
>
> PSALMS 121:3-4

Jake left on a business trip, admonishing her to be sure all the windows and doors were se-cure before she and their daugh-ter, Daisy, went to bed. "We'll be okay," she assured him. "God has always taken care of us, and He knows we need His protec-tion more than ever."

The memory of her words made her smile a bit in retrospect. She wasn't feeling very peaceful when evening actually arrived. As she checked the last door lock, she thought she heard people yelling somewhere down the street, which made her even more tense.

When she reached Daisy's room, she found her sitting in a little ball in the middle of her bed. Her wide eyes told Anna that she had heard the yelling too.

"Mom, do we have to turn out the lights tonight?" Daisy pleaded. Anna had not left the lights on for Daisy since she was four. The bright country moon had provided enough light to wean her away from the night light. But God's lamp, as they had called it, was nowhere to be seen in this smoggy city atmosphere.

"Honey, do you really need it?" Anna asked.

"Yes! I can't see God's lamp tonight. He must have already gone to bed."

"Sweetie, God never sleeps. Even when you can't see His lamp, He's up there watching over you."

"Well," Daisy replied, "as long as God is awake, there is no sense in both of us staying awake!"

As you turn off the lights and climb into bed tonight, your fears may not be the same as Daisy's, but the same truth can comfort you: God is awake! He's always watching over you, ready to protect you from harm.

God is protecting because he is
proactively detecting!

UNKNOWN

NIGHT SOUNDS

The night seems to have different sounds and rhythms than the day. It isn't necessarily that the specific sounds of the night are louder or exclusively belonging to the night, although some are. Rather, it is at night that we seem to hear certain sounds more clearly. It is at night that we are likely to notice

- the ticking of a clock,
- the creak of a stair,
- the chirp of a cricket,
- the barking of a dog,
- the scrape of a twig against the window,
- the clatter of a loose shutter,
- the deep call of a foghorn,
- the wind in the trees,
- the croaking of a frog,
- the opening of a door,
- the strains of music down the hall,
- the whimper of a child, and
- the whispers of a spouse.

It is also at night that we are more prone to listen with our spiritual ears. Frederick Buechner has suggested, "Listen to your life. See it for the fathomless mystery that it is. In the boredom and pain of it no less than in the excitement and gladness: touch, taste, smell your way to the holy and hidden heart of it because in the last analysis all moments are key moments, and life itself is grace." [44]

- Listen to the moment.
- Listen to your thoughts and feelings.
- Listen to your impulses and desires.
- Listen to your longings and fears.
- Listen to the beat of your own heart.
- Listen to God's still small voice in the innermost recesses of your being.

Night is for listening. Listen—and learn—with your spiritual ears, as well as your natural ones.

_____

God has given human beings one tongue
but two ears that we may hear twice as
much as we speak.

UNKNOWN

PRAYING GRANDMOTHERS

For fifty years Sister Agnes and Mrs. Baker had prayed for their nation of Latvia to be freed from Soviet oppression. Most of all, they prayed for the freedom to worship in their Methodist Church in Leipaja. When the atheistic Soviet regime came to power, the enemy invaders took over their church building and turned the sanctuary into a sports hall.

> For the eyes of the Lord run to and fro throughout the whole earth, to shew himself strong in the behalf of them whose heart is perfect toward him.
>
> 2 CHRONICLES 16:9 KJV

Their prayers were answered in 1991, when the oppression came to an end. The Soviets left, and the tiny nation was free. But it needed to be rebuilt, and Sister Agnes and Mrs. Baker were determined to help.

First the two women, now past eighty, talked to a local minister. They said if he would agree to be their pastor, they would be his first members. A church was reborn!

Next they had to regain ownership of the building. That done, they began getting the church ready for worship services. One of the church members undertook painting the twenty-five-foot-high walls. For weeks she mounted scaffolding and painted the walls and ceiling. The tall Palladian windows were cleaned to a bright, gleaming shine, and the wood floor was restored to a rich luster.

Because of careful record keeping by church members, the original church pews were found in storage out in the country. They were returned and put in place for worshipers. Sister Agnes had kept the church pump organ safe in her own home, so she returned it to the sanctuary.

God had been faithful! Lenin had predicted Christianity would die out within a generation. After the grandmothers died, he said, there would be no more Christians left. But he didn't know Sister Agnes and Mrs. Baker and the God they loved!

God wants to show himself strong on your behalf, just as He did for Mrs. Baker and Sister Agnes. Jesus said, "I will build my church; and the gates of Hades will not overcome it" (Matthew 16:18).

You are part of His Church, and He will not let evil triumph over you! No matter what you are facing tonight, have faith that He will bring you through.

Faith is the eye that sees him, the hand
that clings to him, the receiving power
that appropriates him.

FREDERICK JAMES WOODBRIDGE

IN HIS EYES

I n *The Upper Room*, Sandra Palmer Carr describes a touching moment with one of her sons. When her younger son, Boyd, was four years old, she was rocking him in a high-backed wooden rocking chair, as was her habit. But this time he was facing her, straddling her lap with his knees bent.

> The eyes of the Lord are upon the righteous.
>
> PSALM 34:15 KJV

Suddenly, he sat up straight, lifted his head, and stared intensely into her eyes. He became very still, and Sandra stopped rocking. He cupped her face in his little hands and said in a near-whisper, "Mommy, I'm in your eyes."

They stayed that way for several long moments, staring into one another's eyes. The rocking stopped, and the room grew quiet. Then Sandra whispered back, "And I'm in yours." Boyd leaned his head against her contentedly, and they resumed their rocking.

In the days that followed, Boyd would often check to see if his discovery still held true. "Am I still in your eyes, Mommy?" he would ask, reaching up to her. She would pull him close to her so he could look in her eyes and see for himself — he was still there![45]

How can we be assured we are always in God's eyes? The Bible has many, many verses to indicate He is continuously thinking of us, attending to us, and doing all He can to bless us. Certainly, Jesus' death and resurrection are a constant reminder of how dear and precious we are to Him.

One of the best times to stop and see yourself in God's eyes is just before falling asleep. Your Heavenly Father desires to rock you to sleep in His love, letting you stop now and then to call to mind a verse of Scripture that tells you how much you mean to Him.

You should never doubt you are the focus of God's tender care and attention. You can have a grateful and confident heart knowing you are always in his eyes.

The only important decision we have to make is to live with God; he will make the rest.

ANONYMOUS

AFTER THE UPROAR

After the uproar was ceased, Paul called unto him the disciples, and embraced them.

ACTS 20:1 KJV

For a small child, the most comforting place in the world is in the secure arms of his mother or father. It's not really very different for grown-ups. The embrace of caring arms is a wonderful place to be. Even a brief hug from a casual friend can lift one's spirits.

At the end of a busy or frustrating day, "after the uproar has ceased," grown-ups may long for a pair of loving parental arms to assure them everything's going to be all right—to hear a voice that says soothingly, "I'm here, and I'll take care of you."

Take this little poem as a "hug" this evening from One who loves you without measure, and who watches over your every move with tenderness and compassion:

> When the birds begin to worry
> And the lilies toil and spin,
> And God's creatures all are anxious,
> Then I also may begin.
>
> For my Father sets their table,
> Decks them out in garments fine,
> And if He supplies their living,
> Will He not provide for mine?

Just as noisy, common sparrows
Can be found most anywhere —
Unto some just worthless creatures,
If they perish who would care?

Yet our Heavenly Father numbers
Every creature great and small,
Caring even for the sparrows,
Marking when to earth they fall.

If His children's hairs are numbered,
Why should we be filled with fear?
He has promised all that's needful,
And in trouble to be near.

UNKNOWN

Our ground of hope is that God does not
weary of mankind.

RALPH WASHINGTON SOCKMAN

TEA FOR AT LEAST TWO

T he brief respite known as afternoon tea is said to have been the creation of Anna, Duchess of Bedford, in the nineteenth century. At that time the English customarily ate a hearty breakfast, paused for a light lunch at midday, and didn't return to the table until late evening. Understandably hungry long before dinner, the duchess asked to have a small meal served in her private quarters in the late afternoon. Eventually, she invited close friends to share the repast. The sensible custom was quickly adopted throughout England.

> He leadeth me beside the still waters. He restoreth my soul.
>
> PSALMS 23:2-3 KJV

While the Duchess's initiation of teatime was aimed at nourishment of her body, she and the rest of England soon discovered that adding beautiful china and good friends to the occasion also nourished the soul. In fact, the real value of formal teatime lies in its ability to enrich and brighten the everyday routine by stressing the importance of courtesy and friendship.[46]

We are wise to recognize our need for a "spiritual teatime" each day. Even if we have a "hearty breakfast" in the Word each morning, there may be times when the pressures of the day come to bear in late afternoon. Our spirits long for a little peace and refreshment in the presence of our loving Savior. Just as enjoying a muffin with a few sips of tea can give something of a lift to our lagging physical energy level, a quick prayer or the voicing of praise can give our spirit a lift.

Set aside some time in the middle of the afternoon to turn your attention to the beauty of life that the Lord has set before you. Find beauty and comfort in the people around you, the flowers on a table, or simply the delicious aroma of tea brewing. Create a few moments away from the hustle and bustle of your life before returning to the tasks that await you. Give thanks to the Lord for sharing His presence with you.

Gratitude is born in hearts that take time
to count up past mercies.

CHARLES E. JEFFERSON

THAT LOVING TOUCH

Being a flawed human being isn't easy. Around teatime, when our energy is a bit low, we are more likely to recognize all the ways we've failed during the day. Sometimes we wonder how our Heavenly Father puts up with all of our inadequacies.

A minister told of a certain family in his church who had waited a long time for a child. The couple was overjoyed when at last a son was born to them, but they were crushed when they learned he had a severe handicap. Lie would go into extremely violent seizures without warning. Nevertheless, as he grew, they tried to make his life as normal as possible.

> He hath said, I will never leave thee, nor forsake thee.
>
> HEBREWS 13:5 KJV

Whenever the church doors were open, this family could be found in attendance. As time passed, the child developed a deep love for the same Jesus his parents loved, and he counted on Him to bring him through each of his life-threatening episodes.

The minister tells of the father's love as reflected on one particular Sunday:

I remember the father always holding the little boy during worship at our church. I remember one particularly hard seizure when the father gently but firmly held the little guy and went to the back of the sanctuary. There he held him to his chest, gently whispering into his ear. There was no hint of embarrassment or frustration on that father's face. Only calm, deep, abiding love.

That is a picture of our Heavenly Father's love for us. In spite of our deep imperfections, He is not embarrassed to call us His children. He tenderly holds us through the deepest, hardest part of our struggles and whispers words of assurance and encouragement while He clutches us to himself and supports us with His loving care.

He prayeth best, who loveth best,

all things both great and small;

for the dear God who loveth us,

he made and loveth all.

SAMUEL TAYLOR COLERIDGE

THE SYMPATHETIC JEWEL

H ave you ever noticed that those who reject you often seem to lack joy? Have you ever considered that they could be guarded and standoffish because they have been rejected themselves? In fact, their rejection of you may be a defense mechanism.

Sometimes your warm attitude toward them can make all the difference. This is illustrated by the story of a man who visited a jewelry store owned by a friend. His friend showed him magnificent diamonds and other splendid stones. Among these stones the visitor spotted one that seemed quite lusterless. Pointing to it, he said, "That stone has no beauty at all."

His friend put the gem in the hollow of his hand and closed his fingers tightly around it. In a few moments, he uncurled his fingers.

What a surprise! The entire stone gleamed with the splendor of a rainbow. "What have you done to it?" asked the astonished man.

His friend answered, "This is an opal. It is what we

"But I say unto you, Love your enemies, bless them that curse you, do good to them that hate you, and pray for them which despitefully use you, and persecute you . . ."

MATTHEW 5:44 KJV

call the sympathetic jewel. It only needs to be gripped with the human hand to bring out its full beauty."

People are very much like opals. Without warmth, they become dull and colorless. But "grasp" them with the warmth and love of God, and they come alive with personality and humor. Unlike chameleons who simply adapt to their background, people who feel embraced by the love of God and His people come alive with colorful personalities all their own.

It's difficult to embrace those who have rejected us. However, if we can see beyond the facade they have erected to the potential inside them, we can be the healing hands of Jesus extended to them . . . and bring healing to ourselves in the process.

Nobody will know what you mean by
saying that "God is love" unless you act it
as well.

LAWRENCE PEARSALL JACKS

A TIME FOR EVERYTHING

There is a
right time
for
everything.

ECCLESIASTES
3:1 TLB

Most Christians are familiar with the passage in Ecclesiastes that tells us, "To everything there is a season." Consider this modern-day version of the same message:

To everything there is a time . . .

A time to wind up, and a time to wind down;

A time to make the call, and a time to unplug the phone;

A time to set the alarm, and a time to sleep in;

A time to get going, and a time to let go.

A time for starting new projects, and a time for celebrating victories;

A time for employment, and a time for retirement;

A time for overtime, and a time for vacation;

A time for making hay, and a time for lying down on a stack of it to watch the clouds go by.

A time for making plans, and a time for implementing them;

A time for seeing the big picture, and a time for mapping out details;

A time for working alone, and a time for involving others.

A time for building morale, and a time for growing

profits;

A time for giving incentives, and a time for granting rewards;

A time for giving advice, and a time for taking it.

No matter what your situation or environment, the Lord has designed a rhythm for life that includes rest and exertion. If you maintain this balance, you'll likely find there is plenty of "time for everything" that is truly beneficial to you!

What time is it?

Time to do well, time to live better, give

up that grudge, answer that letter, speak

the kind word to sweeten a sorrow, do

that kind deed you would leave 'till

tomorrow.

UNKNOWN

REWARDS

The writer of Hebrews encourages us to believe two things about God: First, He exists, and second, He is a "rewarder of those who diligently seek Him" (Hebrews 11:6 NKJV). Among the rewards for those who seek the Lord are reconciliation to God, forgiveness of sins, peace of heart and mind, provision and help, and power to overcome evil. All of these are wonderful rewards . . . but they are also intangible ones.

> Surely there is a reward for the righteous.
>
> PSALM 58:11
> NKJV

Like children who live in a material world, we often desire "God with skin on." We long to see, feel, and touch our rewards. This is certainly true in the workplace. We desire the rewards of promotions, praise, and raises. It is also true at home. We long to feel appreciation, to be hugged and kissed, and to receive tangible gifts from our loved ones.

Is there a link between the intangible rewards that come from God and the tangible rewards of the "real world"? There may be! Research has revealed that those who have less stress in their lives—a by-product of peace, forgiveness, reconciliation, and spiritual power—enjoy these rewards:

- Fewer illnesses, doctor's appointments, need for medication, and overall health care expense.

- Fewer repairs on appliances and machinery. Apparently when we are at peace on the inside, we use machines with more precision and patience. We break things with less frequency.

• Fewer automobile accidents. When we are feeling peace and harmony with God and people, we are less aggressive and more careful in driving.

What *doesn't* happen to us can be just as much a reward as receiving a present or a hug.

Diligently seek the Lord today. Make your relationship with Him your number one concern. And enjoy the rewards He will bring your way!

God is never found accidentally.

A. W. TOZER

COPING SKILLS

How we handle delays tells us a lot about ourselves. How do you handle a traffic jam when you left the house already late for work? What do you do when your flight is delayed because of mechanical difficulty or bad weather? How do you respond when the register in your checkout lane runs out of tape just as you get to the head of the line? Can you take a deep breath and enjoy a five-minute break at the railroad crossing when the guard rail goes down to allow a train to pass?

> My times are in your hand.
>
> PSALM 31:15
> NRSV

Consider how one man handled a delay. Just as the light turned green at the busy intersection, his car stalled in heavy traffic. He tried everything he knew to get the car started again, but all his efforts failed. The chorus of honking behind him put him on edge, which only made matters worse.

Finally he got out of his car and walked back to the first driver and said, "I'm sorry, but I can't seem to get my car started. If you'll go up there and give it a try, I'll stay here and blow your horn for you."

Things rarely go as smoothly as we would like, and we don't usually schedule ourselves any extra time just in case something goes wrong.

The ability to accept disappointments, delays, and setbacks with a pleasant, generous spirit is a gift of graciousness that comes from one who has received grace from others in pressured circumstances. Life is a series of choices, and no matter what situation we are in, we always have the freedom to choose how we are going to respond.

Refuse to get out of sorts the next time your schedule gets interrupted or turned upside down. Pray for strength to remain calm, cheerful, relaxed, and refreshed in the midst of the crisis. And always remember: God's plans for you are not thwarted by delays!

Sometimes God's appointments come
from life's disappointments!

UNKNOWN

SEVENTY TIMES SEVEN

W hen one boy hit another during Sunday-school class, the teacher's aid took the offending child outside for discipline. She then assigned a crafts project to the rest of the class so she could talk to the child who had been hit. "You need to forgive Sam for hitting you, Joey," she said.

> "Forgive, and you will be forgiven."
>
> LUKE 6:37 NKJV

"Why?" Joey asked. "He's mean. He doesn't deserve any forgiveness."

The teacher said, "The disciples of Jesus may have felt that same way. They asked Jesus how many times they had to forgive someone who was mean to them, and Jesus said seventy times seven." (See Matthew 18:21-22.) Joey sat thoughtfully, and the teacher continued, "Do you know how many times that is, Joey?"

Joey had just learned how to multiply, so he took a nearby pencil and piece of paper and worked this math puzzle. Upon getting his answer, he looked up at the teacher and said in shock, "Do you mean to tell me that Sam is going to hit me 489 more times! I'm going to be black and blue for forgiving him all year!"

That's the way many of us may feel—perpetually pummeled by those who continue to hurt or wound us, inadvertently or willfully, day in and day out. Memories also can haunt us, causing unforgiveness to spring up again and again. What are we to do? Forgive! It may take 490 times of saying under our breath or in our hearts, "I forgive you," but forgive we must if we are to be free on the inside.

To forgive does not mean another person's behavior has not hurt us or that they were justified in their actions. A wrong may have been committed. But forgiving means saying, "I choose to let you go. I will not hold the memory of this inside me. I will not seek revenge."

In forgiving some people or memories, we may very well have to "let go" 490 times. But in the end, we will be free, and the other person will be in God's hands.

"I can forgive, but I cannot forget," is only another way of saying, "I cannot forgive."

HENRY WARD BEECHER

LIGHTENING UP

Are you a strict constructionist or a loose constructionist? These terms came into vogue after the United States Constitution was adopted. A strict constructionist takes the document exactly as it is; a loose constructionist sees room for different applications and interpretations.

When it comes to your daily schedule, are you strict or loose? Do you refuse to deviate from your to-do list, or are you easygoing enough to shift gears when opportunity knocks at your door?

A young mother with four small children had given up on ever finding time for a break. Her husband frequently worked overtime, which meant she was totally responsible for taking care of the house and the children. She had decided the only way to make it all work was to be as rigid as a drill sergeant.

Certain chores had to be performed at a set time each day and on certain days of the week. If not, she felt pressured to make up for lost time by staying up later or getting up earlier . . . which drained her energy, made her cranky, and resulted in getting less done the following day.

> Blessed be the Lord, for he has made marvelous his lovingkindness to me in a besieged city.
>
> PSALM 31:21 NASB

One afternoon, her five-year-old daughter came into the kitchen, where she was planning dinner. "Come to my tea party," she said, a big smile on her face. Normally, Mom would have said, "Not now; I'm busy." But that day she had a flashback to her own five-year-old self inviting her mother to a tea party and being turned down.

Instead of saying no, she helped her daughter put together a tray containing a plate of cookies, some sandwiches cut into bite-size pieces, a small pot of tea, sugar and cream, her best teaspoons, and a couple of linen napkins. The two oldest children were at school. The youngest was napping. The house was quiet, and the young mother couldn't remember when she'd enjoyed a cup of tea so much.

———————————

Drop thy still dews of quietness, till all
our strivings cease; take from our souls
the strain and stress, and let our ordered
lives confess the beauty of thy peace.

JOHN GREENLEAF WHITTIER

FIRE!

It's usually about teatime when we realize that the clock's been moving faster than we have. So we break into a mental sprint to see if we can beat the clock to the day's finish line. It's usually about this time of day when everyone and everything needs immediate attention. Sometimes we end the day thinking all we did for the last few hours was "put out brush fires." Consequently, the primary objectives of the day stand waiting for attention.

> Be pleased, O Lord, to deliver me: O Lord, make haste to help me!
>
> PSALM 40:13 NKJV

With the usual candor of children, one kindergartner shed some light on this late-afternoon dilemma. He was on a class field trip to fire station to take a tour and learn about fire safety. The fireman explained what to do in case of a fire. "First, go to the door and feel it to see if it's hot. Then, if you smell or see smoke coming in around the door, fall to your knees. Does anyone know why you ought to fall to your knees?"

The little boy piped up and said, "Sure! To start praying to ask God to get you out of this mess!"

What a good idea for those brush fires that break out in the heat the day! If we mentally and spiritually fall to our knees, we move our thoughts to God's presence around us and His authority over the circumstances we are facing.

Falling to our knees puts us beneath the "smoke" of confusion and enables us to breathe in gulps of reason, calm, and clarity. We are in a better position to see a way out of the burning room and move in an efficient and productive direction.

By giving us knees on which to fall, God has already answered our prayer for help. Bowing down for prayer reminds us who has ultimate control over the situation, and it puts us in communication with Him. He allows us to see how to rescue the day from the afternoon crunch.

Sometimes your teatime becomes a "falling on your knees" time!

Speak to him thou for he hears, and spirit
with spirit can meet—closer is he than
breathing, and nearer than hands and feet.

ALFRED, LORD TENNYSON

THE KEY INGREDIENT

"He's coming home, honey!" Caroline shouted to her husband.

Their son, Brad, had left home for college a few months earlier, leaving their home much too quite and empty. The phone hardly ever rang, and the doorbell remained silent. His absence took a toll on Caroline's emotions, causing her to retreat from the things that she always enjoyed.

Now he was coming to visit. Excitedly, Caroline changed the sheets on Brad's cold bed, remembering the many nights she knelt beside him as he said his bedtime prayers. For the last few months, she had wished so many times that she could kiss him goodnight before retiring for the evening. After she fluffed his pillow and straightened up his bedroom, she breezed into the kitchen to bake his favorite dessert—a buttermilk pound cake.

> This is the day the Lord has made; let us rejoice and be glad in it.
>
> PSALM 118:24

All the ingredients were on hand, and she almost had the recipe memorized. She measured them out carefully and made every effort to mix it as directed, but before all the flour was mixed in, the phone rang. After a brief conversation, she returned to the cake. She poured the batter into the baking pans and hurriedly placed them in the preheated oven.

About halfway through the baking time, she looked

into the mixing bowl. Oh, no! She had left out a large portion of the flour! A quick glance into the oven confirmed her fears; the cake was not rising. She was so disappointed. Despite her good intentions, she had left out most of an important ingredient. The case might taste okay, but it was flat and gooey.

Life is a lot like that cake. Some experiences may seem to be good and offer happiness, but without Christ, the most important element of life is missing. Do you have all the ingredients for a fulfilled life?

Be simple; take our Lord's hand and walk through things.

FATHER ANDREW

THE PERSON IN THE MIRROR

A s Christ's nature grows within us, the selfish nature with which we were born begins to recede into the background. Our attitudes toward others change along with our behavior.

One writer notes the following:

Some of us are so full of ourselves that we cannot see Christ in all His beauty.

Some years ago, when I was away on a preaching appointment, my wife and little daughter stayed at the home of a friend. On the bedroom wall just over the head of the bed in which they slept there was a picture of the Lord Jesus, which was reflected in the large mirror of the dressing table standing in the bay of the bedroom window.

When my little daughter woke on her first morning there, she saw the picture reflected in the mirror and exclaimed, "Oh, Mummy, I can see Jesus through the mirror!" Then she quickly kneeled up to take a better look, but in doing so brought her own body between the picture and the mirror, so that instead of seeing the

Looking unto Jesus the author and finisher of our faith; who for the joy that was set before him endured the cross, despising the shame, and is set down at the right hand of the throne of God.

HEBREWS 12:2 KJV

picture of Jesus reflected, she now saw herself.

So she lay down again, and again she saw the picture of Jesus. She was up and down several times after that with her eyes fixed on the mirror.

Finally, she said, "Mummy, when I can't see myself, I can see Jesus; but every time I see myself, I don't see Him."

When self fills our vision, we do not see Jesus. This afternoon, when the events of the day and your personal concerns are heavy on your mind, turn your eyes to Jesus. Then see if you don't feel transported from the cross you have been bearing to His throne in Heaven!

Before us is a future all unknown, a path untrod; beside us a friend well-loved and known—that friend is God.

UNKNOWN

REFERENCES

Unless otherwise indicated, all Scripture quotations are taken from the *Holy Bible, New International Version®. NIV®*. Copyright ©1973, 1978, 1984 by International Bible Society. Used by permission of Zondervan Publishing House. All rights reserved.

Scripture quotations marked KJV are taken from the *King James Version* of the Bible.

Scripture quotations marked NKJV are taken from *The New King James Version*. Copyright ©1979, 1980, 1982, Thomas Nelson, Inc.

Scripture quotations marked RSV are taken from *The Revised Standard Version Bible*, copyright ©1946, Old Testament section copyright ©1952 by the Division of Christian Education of the National Council of the Churches of Christ in the United States of America. Used by permission.

Scripture quotations marked AMP are taken from *The Amplified Bible*. Old Testament copyright ©1965, 1987 by Zondervan Corporation, Grand Rapids, Michigan. New Testament copyright ©1958, 1987 by The Lockman Foundation, La Habra, California. Used by permission.

Scripture quotations marked NASB are taken from the *New American Standard Bible*. Copyright © The Lockman Foundation 1960, 1962, 1963, 1968, 1971, 1972, 1973, 1975, 1977, 1995. Used by permission.

Verses marked TLB are taken from *The Living Bible* ©1971. Used by permission of Tyndale House Publishers,

Inc., Wheaton, Illinois 60189.

Scriptures marked NCV are quoted from *The Holy Bible, New Century Version*, copyright ©1987, 1988, 1991 by Word Publishing, Dallas, Texas 75039. Used by permission.

Scripture quotations marked NRSV are from the *New Revised Standard Version of the Bible*, copyright ©1989 by The Division of Christian Education of the National Council of the Churches of Christ in the USA. Used by permission.

ENDNOTES

[1]*The New Dictionary of Thoughts*, Tryon Edwards, ed. (NY: Standard Book Company, 1963) p. 506.

[2]Richard Blanchard, "Fill My Cup, Lord," *Chorus Book* (Dallas: Word, Inc., 1971).

[3]Philip E. Howard Jr., *New Every Morning* (Grand Rapids, MI: Zondervan, 1969) pp. 12-13.

[4]Charles Swindoll, *The Finishing Touch* (Dallas: Word Publishing, 1994) p. 274.

[5]Helen Keller, *The Open Door* (NY: Doubleday & Co., 1957) pp. 12-13.

[6]Lloyd John Ogilvie, *Silent Strength for My Life* (Eugene, OR: Harvest House Publishers, 1990) p. 32.

[7]Reuben P. Job and Norman Shawchuck, *A Guide to Prayer* (Nashville, TN: The Upper Room, 1983) p. 234.

[8]*San Luis Obispo Telegraph-Tribune* (January 31, 1996) B-3.

[9]Donald S. Whitney, *Spiritual Disciplines for the Christian Life* (Colorado Springs: NavPress, 1991) p. 37

[10]Denis Waitley and Reni Witt, *The Joy of Working* (NY: Dodd Mead and Company, 1985) p. 253.

[11]*Pacific Discovery* (Summer 1990) pp. 23-24.

[12]Walter B. Knight, *Knight's Master Book of 4,000 Illustrations* (Grand Rapids, MI: William B. Eerdmans Publishing Co., 1956) p. 93.

[13]Denis Waitley and Reni L. Witt, *The Joy of Working* (NY: Dodd, Mead and Company, 1985) pp. 23-24.

[14]*The Message*, Eugene H. Peterson, ed. (Colorado Springs: Navpress, 1993, 1994, 1995) pp. 722-723.

[15]Gary Johnson, *Reader's Digest* (September 1991) pp. 164-165.

[16]*The Methodist Reporter* (November/December 1995)

editorial section.

[17]Charles R. Swindoll, *The Finishing Touch* (Dallas: Word Publishing, 1994) pp. 186-187.

[18]*Reader's Digest* (December 1991) pp. 96-100.

[19]*A Guide to Prayer for All God's People*, Rueben P. Job and Norman Shawchuck, eds. (Nashville, TN: Upper Room Books, 1990) pp. 326-328.

[20]Marjorie Holmes, *Lord, Let Me Love* (NY: Doubleday) pp. 104-105.

[21]Author unknown.

[22]Mike Nichols, "Self-Esteem," *The Complete Book of Everyday Christianity*, Robert Banks and R. Paul Stevens, eds. (Downers Grove, IL: Intervarsity Press, 1997) p. 872.

[23]*Christianity Today* (December 9, 1996) Vol. 40, No. 14, p. 80.

[24]P. W. Alexander, "Christmas at Home," *Writing for Change: A Community Reader* (San Francisco, CA: McGraw-Hill, Inc., 1995) pp. 100-101.

[25]Ibid. p. 102.

[26]Bill Cosby, *Fatherhood* (New York; Berkley Books, 1986).

[27]George Sweeting, *Who Said That?* (Chicago: Moody Press, 1995).

[28]*Masterpieces of Religious Verse*, James Dalton Morrison, ed. (NY: Harper &C Brothers Publishers, 1948).

[29]Nanette Thorsen-Snipes, *After the Storm: Learning to Abide* (Star Books, 1990).

[30]Ginger Galloway, *Guideposts* (August 1997).

[31]Hannah Whitall Smith, *The Christian's Secret of a Happy Life* pp. 38-40.

[32]Herman W. Gockel, *Give Your Life a Lift* (St. Louis: Concordia Publishing House, 1968) p. 114.

[33]Billy Graham, *Unto the Hills: A Devotional Treasury* (Waco, TX: Word Books, 1986) p. 158.

[34]Ibid., p. 223.

[35]*A Moment a Day*, Mary Beckwith and Kathi Mills, eds. (Ventura, CA: Regal Books, 1988) p. 25.

[36]Ibid., p. 174.

[37]Ibid., p. 184.

[38]Herman W. Gockel, *Give Your Life a Lift* (St. Louis: Concordia Publishing House, 1968) pp. 38-39.

[39]Ibid, p. 56.

[40]*Prevention* (March 1996) pp. 25- 26.

[41]*The Treasury of Inspirational Quotations & Illustrations*, E. Paul Hovey, ed. (Grand Rapids, MI: Baker Books, 1994) p. 168.

[42]*The Treasure Chest*, Brian Culhane, ed. (San Francisco: HarperCollins, 1995) p. 92.

[43]Ibid., p. 94.

[44]Ibid., p. 146.

[45]*The Upper Room* (May-June 1996) p. 15.

[46]Patricia Gentry, *Teatime Collections* (San Ramon, CA: Chevron Chemical Co., 1988) p. 5.

Additional copies of this book and other titles in the
Quiet Moments with God Devotional series are available
from your local bookstore or online.

Quiet Moments with God
Quiet Moments with God for Couples
Quiet Moments with God for Women
Quiet Moments with God for Teachers
Quiet Moments with God for Teens